Chesi Shah

D0933214

REVIVAL

in Brownsville

*Pensacola, Pentecostalism,
and the Power of American Revivalism*

STEVE RABEY

THOMAS NELSON PUBLISHERS
Nashville

Copyright © 1998 by Steve Rabey

Published in association with the literary agency of Alive Communications, 1465 Kelly Johnson Blvd., Suite 320, Colorado Springs, CO 80920.

All rights reserved. Written permission must be secured from the publisher to use or reproduce any part of this book, except for brief quotations in critical reviews or articles.

Published in Nashville, Tennessee, by Thomas Nelson, Inc., Publishers.

The Bible version used in this publication is THE NEW KING JAMES VERSION. Copyright © 1979, 1980, 1982, 1990, Thomas Nelson, Inc., Publishers.

Cover and interior photos courtesy of Cathy Wood.

Library of Congress Cataloging-in-Publication Data

Rabey, Steve.
    Revival in Brownsville : Pensacola, Pentecostalism, and the power of American revivalism / Steve Rabey.
      p. cm.
    Includes bibliograchical references
    ISBN 0-7852-7498-7 (pbk.)
    1. Brownsville Assembly of God (Pensacola, Fla.) 2. Revivals—Florida—Pensacola. I. Title.
BX8765.5.Z7P467   1998
289'.9'0975999—dc21   98-44550
                                            CIP

Printed in the United States of America.

1 2 3 4 5 6 QPV 03 02 01 00 99 98

Contents

PART I

The Making of a Movement

Ever since June 1995, crowds have been thronging to evening revival meetings at Brownsville Assembly of God in Pensacola, Florida.

CHAPTER ONE

Pilgrimage to Pensacola:

Why Millions of People
Have Traveled to One Florida Church

It is a warm spring evening as the sun begins to set on the Gulf Coast town of Pensacola, Florida. But as the hot southern sun gradually goes dim, the sense of anticipation brightens among the thousands of people lined up to get into a large, modern brick building in the city's lower-class Brownsville neighborhood. After all, some of them have been waiting here since before the sun rose this morning.

From a distance, the long line and the packed parking lot resemble a throng eagerly waiting to hear a popular performer's sold-out concert, or fans rooting for the home team at a hotly contested game, or perhaps shoppers saving a bundle at an acclaimed flea market.

Most of these folks, however, are not concerned with such worldly matters, even though some music, some cheering, and maybe even some saving are in store for them.

Drawing closer, you can hear people singing or praying together in small groups. Others sit in lawn chairs, seemingly lost in private reveries. And some chat with their neighbors in line as if they are old-time friends, which is a bit odd, because few of them have ever laid eyes on each other before. While some come from around the corner or down the street, others have come from the other side of the globe.

Ask why they have made the pilgrimage to Pensacola, and you will hear variations on the theme of hunger for a vital and personal relationship with God.

"I want more of Him," says a forty-something single mother from Georgia, looking heavenward as she speaks, and gesturing with her upturned hands in a motion of invocation.

"I know God is here in power," says a balding German pastor, who is hoping an infusion of spiritual energy will fill his parched soul and give him a surplus with which to feed his hungry flock back home.

Then, about an hour before the service begins, Ellis Lee, one of the security guards who has been working here since the crowds first began arriving in 1995, turns on his megaphone and gives the pilgrims a few final instructions. "We're just about ready to open the doors," he says. "Please stay in a single-file line."

Turning to me, Lee says, "These are very dedicated people. They have to be, to stay in this line all day. And they're hungry for the Word." A member of a nearby African Methodist Episcopal church, Lee has seen days when the mass of hungry souls was eight thousand strong and four blocks long. He has no doubt that the event drawing all these people to Pensacola is "a move of the Lord." Watching the throng, he says, "These people are seeking something, and they are finding it."

As the metal-and-glass doors swing open and the crowd begins to file into the auditorium-sized sanctuary of the Brownsville Assembly of God, moms, ministers, and many more feel they are entering sacred space. As they walk down the wide carpeted aisles—aisles that in a few hours' time will be filled with the lifeless bodies of stricken worshipers—some tread lightly, as if they are walking on holy ground.

Unfortunately, it's a rare day that everyone standing in line gains admission to the sanctuary. Most will be diverted to a variety of overflow rooms, where they will watch the proceedings on big TV screens. Some will wind up in a chapel building across the street. Others file into the church's choir room and cafeteria. Another fifteen hundred squeeze into a large tent. And on most nights, hundreds more are told to come back the next day. Some of these disappointed pilgrims pledge to be back in line before dawn.

Crowds like these have been coming to the Brownsville church for more than three years now. All told, more than 2.5 million people have visited the church's Wednesday-through-Saturday evening revival services, where they sang rousing worship music and heard old-fashioned sermons on sin and salvation. After the sermons were over, hundreds of thousands accepted the invitation to leave their seats and rush forward to a large area in front of the stage-like altar. Here, they "get right with God." For some that's a private matter, shared only with a few family members and friends. Others publicly testify to God's work in their lives. More than two hundred thousand people have signed "decision cards" indicating they made an initial commitment to Christ, or renewed a faith that had grown cold long ago.

Untold thousands have hit the carpet, where they either writhe in ecstasy or lie stone-still in a state resembling a coma, sometimes remaining flat on the floor for hours at a time. Some participants call the experience being "slain in the Spirit." Others simply refer to receiving the touch of God. Regardless of what they call it, these people are putting the "roll" back in "holy roller."

The fervor being experienced at Brownsville has fanned the flames of renewal in dozens of churches in the Assemblies of God—a worldwide denomination that was itself spawned by the pentecostal revival that ignited at Azusa Street in the early years of this century. In recent decades the Assemblies' fervor had cooled, and its membership had plateaued. But Brownsville has helped renew and reinvigorate hundreds of the denomination's congregations.

And it is not just churches in the Assemblies of God that have been touched. Thousands of pastors from around the world have come to Pensacola to attend services and special pastors' conferences. Clergy in Methodist, Baptist, and Catholic congregations say they are experiencing a newfound enthusiasm for worship, a deeper commitment to living a disciplined Christian life, and a renewed emphasis on evangelism.

Often, pastors make the pilgrimage to Pensacola after some of their church members have returned from Brownsville renewed and revived. Michael Winfree, who attends Coastal Christian Center in North Myrtle Beach, South Carolina, says he has been to Brownsville five times. Other church members have made the trip with him, and now the entire church is experiencing a growing spiritual intensity.

"The preaching here comes directly at you about getting the sin out of your life," says Michael. "It's powerful, and it has turned our church around."

Reporters from newspapers, magazines, and network news programs have also flocked to Florida, following the crowds and filing hundreds of articles about what is happening there, most of them positive portrayals of a back-to-basics approach to Christianity that has powerfully changed thousands of lives.

Drunks are giving up the bottle. Prostitutes are giving up the profession. Sex addicts are giving up their videos and magazines. Couch potatoes are giving up HBO. Gays and lesbians are giving up same-sex relationships. And a whole bunch of folks are giving up religion-as-usual for an intense lifestyle of holiness and Holy Spirit power that supporters say rivals some of the more phenomenal stories from the New Testament book of Acts.

Of course, not everyone has been so moved. For example, in "Maybe Angels," a song about current spiritual trends, musician Sheryl Crow described a visit to Brownsville: "All I found was a bunch of holy rollers." But many who have visited the revival have been revived.

"God is moving," says Steve Hill, whose evangelistic messages helped spawn the Brownsville phenomenon. A former drug addict now determined to tell the world about the amazing grace that turned his own life around, Hill's no-holds-barred zeal for saving souls has sustained him through the course of more than seven hundred high-energy sermons and lengthy post-sermon prayer marathons, some of which have stretched on until one or two in the morning.

Hill and many, many others have no doubt that what is happening in Pensacola is the real thing—a Holy Ghost revival, a sovereign move of God granted by divine dispensation and designed to restore traditional values in America and renew the church around the globe.

Others, however, are not so sure.

Ready for Revival

For centuries, Christian believers around the world have talked about, prayed for, and participated in something known as revival, which for now, at least, we can define as a surprising and supernatural period that brings about the renewal of church members and the salvation of unbelievers. (I'll talk more precisely about what revival is in Chapter 3.)

Whatever the term may mean, revival is a hot topic these days. Bill Bright, founder of Campus Crusade for Christ, regularly hosts events that encourage America's Christian leaders to pray and fast for nationwide repentance and prayer, the subject of his 1995 book, *The Coming Revival*. Stand in the Gap, the event that brought hundreds of thousands of men to Washington, D.C., in 1997, was designed to encourage nationwide renewal and was coordinated by a Promise Keepers executive with the title of "vice president for revival and spiritual awakening."

Canadian pastor Henry Blackaby, whose *Experiencing God* book has been used in nearly twenty denominations and sold more than two million copies, leads Experiencing God Through Revival conferences. And pollster George Barna, in his 1998 book, *The Second Coming of the Church,* says that congregations face two choices: spiritual revival or growing obsolescence.

Today millions of believers in thousands of churches and hundreds of parachurch organizations in dozens of countries are teaching about, praying for, and getting ready for revival.

Surprisingly, there is nothing new about that. Revival has been a recurring theme in the life of the church for twenty centuries, and it has been a major preoccupation of many believers. In the United States, where historians speak of at least two Great Awakenings and a number of lesser spiritual outbreaks, revivalism has had a profound impact on the course of national history, both before and after the American Revolution.

Throughout church history revival has happened in a variety of places, taken a variety of forms, and caused a variety of results in both the church and the larger society. Yet one universal truth has emerged: Today, as always, claims of revival inevitably lead to conflict and controversy.

Critics typically charge that revival emphasizes subjective feeling over objective faith; that it downplays trusted ecclesiastical authorities and raises up new and untested laypeople and charismatic leaders; and that it is noisy but ultimately insignificant, producing little in the way of positive, lasting spiritual fruit. The very things revival advocates ascribe to an extraordinary work of God, others chalk up to some combination of social anxiety, human manipulation, mass delusion, or demonic deception. And both sides bolster their assertions with a variety of biblical proof texts, as well as quotes from the writings of earlier revival leaders, such as New England divine Jonathan Edwards, who was both a participant in and observer of America's fabled Great Awakening.

Contemporary critics follow in the footsteps of American author Sinclair Lewis, whose novel *Elmer Gantry*, written in the

1920s, skewered revivalism with relentless fury. In 1960 the controversial novel was made into an even more controversial movie. The film won three Academy Awards, including one for Burt Lancaster, who turned in a riveting performance as the corrupt and conniving title character. The film opens with the following words emblazoned on the screen, and these words still speak for many today:

> We believe that certain aspects of Revivalism can bear examination—that the conduct of some revivalists makes a mockery of the traditional beliefs and practices of organized Christianity!
>
> We believe that everyone has a right to worship according to his conscience, but Freedom of Religion is not license to abuse the faith of the people!

Today Christian thinkers remain divided over what revival is, what it looks like, and whether or not it is happening at Pensacola. Some longtime Brownsville members have left the church in disgust at what they have seen. Some pastors in the Assemblies of God have raised questions about the way their denomination has embraced the revival. And even the hometown newspaper, the *Pensacola News Journal,* has published not one, but two investigative series debunking the so-called revival.

Farther away from Pensacola, some Christian leaders call what is happening at Brownsville a "counterfeit revival," saying it provides evidence not of God's grandeur but our society's susceptibility to spiritual sensationalism. And while many people say they have been spiritually transformed at Brownsville, others say they were untouched, or even harmed by the church's newfound intensity. There have even been published charges that Brownsville's leaders orchestrated the revival in order to grow wealthy from it, a charge they vehemently deny.

Michael L. Brown is no casual observer. He is a gung-ho

supporter of what is often called "the Pensacola Outpouring." He has prayed for and written about revival for years, and serves as president of the Brownsville Revival School of Ministry, an institution currently training more than a thousand students.

Although not deterred by criticism, Brown has probably spent more time than anyone else at Brownsville defending the revival's theology and practical results against its critics. While he admits he has learned something from some of the more thoughtful naysayers, he says others are too angry and mean-spirited to be constructive.

"I believe people tend to sanitize past revivals and demonize present revivals," Brown says. "When a baby is being born, things are a little bloody and messy, there's a whole lot of noise, and there are a lot of doctors running around. But that doesn't mean the child isn't strong and on its way to a healthy life."

A Reader's Guide to This Book

Revival is an important and complex subject that forces us to consider how God deals with humanity and with the church. For example:

- In what ways, if any, does God renew and revive the church?
- How does one distinguish the divine from the devilish or the merely human in any work of God? Or to ask it another way, what is the best way to tell the difference between the truly holy and everything else, be it hype or hooey?
- And what carries with it the greater danger of offending God and embarrassing the church before a watching world: an enthusiastic, emotional encounter with God that sometimes gets too carried away; or a deadly decorum that may squelch the very Spirit that gives the church its life?

This book will not provide definitive answers to any of these urgent questions, all of which are largely influenced by one's own religious background and theological presuppositions. But, hopefully, readers will get enough information and interpretation to help them make a more informed determination about what is happening in Pensacola, and how this and other renewal movements fit—or don't fit—into God's plan for the church.

No single book can do everything, so here are the things we'll focus on in this one.

A Fair Report

Goal number one is providing an objective and balanced report of the events that have unfolded at Brownsville, including firsthand accounts of the revival services, the messages preached there, and the ways in which people have responded to it all.

Profiles of Leaders

There will be one chapter each about the five men who have had the greatest impact on the shape and direction of the revival: evangelist Steve Hill, pastor John Kilpatrick, worship leader Lindell Cooley, school president Michael Brown, and youth minister Richard Crisco, each of whom has written at least one book of his own on the revival. The goal of these chapters is to help readers understand something about the revival's movers and shakers, and to show how they have changed and been changed by the revival over the past four years.

Mini-Profiles of Revival-Goers

Sandwiched in between the book's twelve chapters are eleven brief profiles of people whose lives have been changed at Brownsville. I thoroughly enjoyed talking to these people, who represent just a tiny portion of the thousands of people for whom visits to Pensacola have been truly transformational.

Context

The chapter you're reading now and the two that follow are intended to explain the background of the Brownsville revival, and to fit the whole phenomenon into the larger contexts of biblical and church history. In these and later chapters, we will compare and contrast the Pensacola revival with both earlier and contemporary renewal movements. In examining how the preaching of Brownsville's Steve Hill measures up to that of the Great Awakening's George Whitefield, for example, or how the music of Lindell Cooley is in some ways inspired by that of Isaac Watts and Charles Wesley, I am merely trying to provide highlights of church history that may help readers have a broader perspective on what is happening today. I am not arguing that future generations will esteem Brownsville's leaders as highly as we do Whitefield and other pillars of the faith.

Admittedly, this effort will be superficial and imperfect. The resource section at the end of the book will help readers pursue some of these issues to a more satisfying extent than is possible here.

Lessons to Apply

Many of the chapters will include an application component in which readers will hear from Brownsville leaders about some of the lessons they have learned during the past few tumultuous years. These sections will help believers pursue true revival with greater understanding, while avoiding some of revivalism's more common excesses.

Critical Analysis

It won't be until the book's third and final section that we begin discussing some of the hard questions that need to be asked about Brownsville, or any movement that claims divine inspiration. Here we will examine how the revival has spread to other churches: both inside and out of the Assemblies of God denomination, as well as in America and beyond. In addition, we will take a look at revivalism's disturbing dark side, and explore the often intense disagreements that have separated revival supporters from revival critics for centuries, and continue to do so today. And in the final chapter, we will make some tentative guesses about Brownsville's potential place in the ongoing history of the church as well as its role in the present-day spread of pentecostalism throughout the world.

A Note on Style and Sources

Taking a cue from pioneering revival researcher David Edwin Harrell, who authored the 1975 classic *All Things Are Possible: The Healing and Charismatic Revivals in Modern America*, I have elected to give people the privilege of telling their own stories in their own words. I may not take everything they say at face value, and the reader certainly needn't do so either. But this method gives the clearest picture of people's experiences at the revival, and it eliminates the need for numerous annoying editorial interruptions, or the overuse of words like *alleged* and *claimed*.

The vast majority of the quotes you will read in this book come from the mouths of revival participants themselves. Worshipers were more than happy to talk about how the revival impacted them. And revival leaders graciously granted me interviews and gave me permission to use material from their sermons, lectures, and audio- and videotapes. They also allowed me to quote from books and other materials they have written, and in cases where these materials are used, source information is provided in the text.

So much for preliminaries. Let's begin our exploration in earnest with a more detailed look at exactly what has been going on at Brownsville since one unusual Sunday in June 1995.

Changed Lives

Blown away

Jason Farmer, one of thousands transformed by the Brownsville revival, went from doing dope to serving God.

He Who Is Forgiven Much Loves Much

Jason Farmer is just one of millions who have attended revival services at Brownsville Assembly of God, and just one of hundreds of thousands who have knelt at the church's packed altar. But for Jason, age twenty-two, visiting the revival in November

1996 rescued him from a horrible downward spiral that threatened to snuff out his life.

"It blows me away," he says, his amazement about the transformation that has taken place in his life lighting up his intense blue eyes. "I used to live to get high. Now all I want to do is serve the Lord."

Jason's life was a story about drugs—lots of drugs. But as in many other cases, his was also a story about one young man's desperate attempt to find a sense of happiness, purpose, and self-esteem.

When he first started drinking and smoking marijuana at age twelve, these were merely occasional diversions. But by his senior year in high school, his substance-abuse problems had escalated. Jason spent a good portion of every day blissfully drunk, stoned, or both. "I was having a blast," he says of his days of partying, his nights of sleeping around, and his Sundays of trying to put on a moral facade at church.

After graduating from high school, Jason worked as a well-paid machine operator by day; by night he blew his money and his brains with increasing doses of cocaine and speed. Next he began dealing drugs, which led directly to his consuming more drugs. By age twenty, he says, "drugs had such a grip on me I wasn't even enjoying them any more."

Even then, Jason believed he was in control of his drug use. That illusion was shattered when he began smoking crack cocaine, a dangerous and highly addictive substance he had earlier promised himself he would never touch.

Life was spiraling out of control. His habits were wasting his body and fogging his mind. He got into regular brushes with the law and had two near-fatal car wrecks. And there was constant paranoia that someone would attack him to get at his money and his drugs. He never left the house without a concealed handgun.

It was in the midst of this mess that Jason's mom, who had already attended a few revival services at Brownsville, drove her son from Texas to Pensacola. "God started dealing with me," he says.

Jason hardly remembers anything about Steve Hill's sermon, but he does recall rushing down the aisle when Hill told anyone who wanted to get right with God to come to the church's big altar. There he fell to his knees and wept like the broken man that he was.

"I just cried and cried," he says. "It felt like there was a cleansing going on inside my body, and that everything was getting washed away." And even though Jason says he was addicted to crack, speed, and prescription drugs, "all that got broken at the altar. I still had dreams about doing drugs, but the cravings were gone."

It has been more than two years since Jason gave his life to God that night. He has not touched drugs or alcohol since. Instead, he has gained weight, developed a healthy self-confidence, and earned the respect of his long-suffering parents. He also enrolled in classes at the Brownsville Revival School of Ministry, classes he says are helping him prepare for a life of ministry.

"It's incomprehensible to me where God brought me from and the bondage I was in," says Jason. "God has done so much for me. It's like Jesus says: he who has been forgiven much loves much."

Today Jason shows his love by volunteering long hours at Brownsville revival services, where he serves as an usher on some nights, and on other nights organizes teams of "catchers," revival lingo for young people who cushion folks as they are slain in the Spirit and fall to the carpet.

"This is my 'reasonable service,' to wear myself out for God," he says, "because when I was in the world, I was going just as hard for the devil."

Worship has been enthusiastic, even rowdy, since revival first broke out on Father's Day 1995.

CHAPTER TWO

Revival at Brownsville:

How It Started and How It Has Spread

The Christian faith is anchored in a series of historical events, the most important of which is the resurrection of Christ. Likewise, the revival at Brownsville Assembly of God is anchored in a number of now-celebrated incidents which, according to revival leaders, church members, and millions of visitors from around the world, indicate that God has touched this Florida congregation in unique and powerful ways.

Those who have long been a part of the revival can recite a litany of important milestones, beginning with the Sunday evening prayer meetings that preceded revival by two and a half years, and continuing through the revival's most recent evening services which, though they are in some ways similar to the hundreds of services that preceded them, still remain distinctive and moving.

No event, however, is as memorable and momentous as the day revered as the revival's official launch: June 18, 1995. For those who were there, the event now enshrined as the Father's Day Outpouring is as near and dear to their hearts as the Boston Tea Party and Washington's crossing the Delaware are to diehard American patriots. For the rest of us, the episode was captured on the church's TV cameras, which recorded every second of the extraordinary six-hour event. The video of that service remains one of the most popular revival videos, with thousands of copies sold at ten dollars each. It is also one of the most controversial documents of the revival, since critics see in this embryonic meeting the seeds of all that they would later find objectionable in the whole affair.

Bibles and Boutonnieres

The members of Brownsville Assembly of God, a solid if somewhat staid congregation of two-thousand-plus souls, were not expecting anything unusual that Father's Day morning. Most everyone carried a well-worn King James Version of the Bible into the sanctuary, fully expecting that Pastor John Kilpatrick would unlock some of its myriad mysteries, as he nearly always did when he preached. And many of the men sported colorful carnations, gifts from either loving children or loyal wives in appreciation for these fathers' persistent—if imperfect—attempts to honor the faith's teachings on family values. Those flowers stood out nicely on the men's dark jackets and would be sure to be noticed later at local restaurants, where many of the church families had reservations for lunch.

The first surprise of the morning came when it was learned that the pastor would not be preaching. Suffering from a bout with a common ailment known as clergy burnout, Kilpatrick was still mourning the recent death of his mother. He was especially close to his mother, who had raised him after an alcoholic father had abandoned the family. Since Kilpatrick had already asked an evangelist friend to speak at the church's Sunday evening service, it was no big problem to have the guest speaker take the morning's sermon as well.

Evangelist Steve Hill just about never turns down an opportunity to tell anyone who will listen about the messages of salvation through Jesus Christ and submission to God. A former drug addict who experienced a dramatic conversion at the age of twenty-one, Hill had spent the last twenty-three years of his life communicating the same life-changing message to others. With a passion for lost souls that frequently causes him to break into tears, Hill's evangelistic zeal had taken him around the world from Argentina to Spain to Russia. Now that same zeal had brought him to Brownsville, one of the congregations that had helped finance his missionary endeavors over the years.

After warming up the Father's Day crowd with a few comments about his two-week-old daughter, Kelsey Noel, Hill launched into his sermon. Using a verse from Psalm 77 ("I will remember the works of the LORD") as his jumping-off point, Hill testified to the things God had done for him, including both his own conversion and a more recent spiritual renewal at Holy Trinity Brompton Church, a vibrant Anglican church in the suburbs of London, England, where Hill says he experienced "a tender time with Jesus."

"My heart is full," he said, pacing the church's large stage area. And as he often does, Hill told the crowd that his frequently used hotline to God had been warm with conversation about what was going to happen that day: "God spoke to me about this service . . . and told me that every person who is dry will be drenched by a heavenly rain."

Before he concentrated on the drenching of the devout, Hill offered salvation to the sinful, extending an invitation to those who were spiritually cold, backslidden, or had never known God to come forward and get right with God. "I am a confrontive evangelist," he said, stomping around the pulpit and walking in between the sanctuary's pews at an increasingly hectic pace. "I am not one of those who says, 'Close your eyes and bow your heads' . . . Get up and come right now!"

As Hill pleaded, only half a dozen people came forward. They were met by church volunteers who prayed and counseled with them. Then Hill returned to his divine assignment for the day.

"This is Father's Day," he said, speaking to his audience while listening to the still, small voice of God in his heart. "The Lord is going somewhere, and I'm going with Him."

Hill briefly recounted some of the works of the Lord he had witnessed firsthand while preaching overseas: evangelists in Argentina bringing thousands of people to the altars in a single rally; prayer meetings marked by healings, visions, miracles, and deliverances; and his own experience of spiritual renewal.

"Little did I know how dry I was until God soaked me," he said, describing a meeting in which he received prayer and fell to the ground.

An Invitation to Go Deeper

Soon Hill began describing the spiritual outpourings that had accompanied his own American preaching rallies. Methodists, Baptists, and others who had little exposure to pentecostal or charismatic traditions were coming forward to receive a greater outpouring of the gifts of the Holy Spirit. Was it possible, he asked, that people from more tradition-bound denominations were hungrier for God than those in Hill's own Assemblies of God denomination, which was founded in the fires of revival? "Where's the pentecostals?" he asked the crowd.

Moving and speaking even more rapidly, Hill told his hearers God had shown him that Christians often hinder the work of the Holy Spirit through their complacency, their criticism, and their comfort with religious conventions. With his voice growing louder and more urgent, Hill shouted out the words he had received from God: "'Steve . . . I am spontaneous. I can do anything I want to do, when I want to do it, and the way I want to do it.'"

Translating this divine word into an assignment for his hearers, Hill told them: "Some of us need an experience with the Lord. We need God to touch us. We need the Lord to come upon

us. Some of you need to experience the nearness of the Lord.
Some of you need to experience your nearness to Him."

Then Hill gave his hearers a warning about what would happen next. "Some of you are going to experience the fire of heaven falling on your life." Some, he said, will fall down. Why? "Because they can't stand up." But falling was not necessary to receive God's blessing, and in itself was not a surefire badge of renewal. "Just because someone falls to the ground does not make them spiritual, friends. But there's nothing wrong with it."

Next, Hill invited anyone wanting to experience the refreshing of God to come forward. Unlike the unenthusiastic response to his earlier invitation, nearly a thousand people—about half of the congregation—left the confines of their pews and streamed forward, filling the large area in front of the pulpit, clogging the aisles with pleading and praying. As a pianist and a handful of singers played gospel choruses, Hill gave a final warning before he descended from the pulpit to begin praying with them one by one.

"We're going to start praying, and after this, I'm no longer responsible."

Bounding from the stage, Hill went from one person to another, touching them on their foreheads or their necks and repeatedly shouting the words, "Jesus!" "Now!" "Fire!" and "More!" Some fell down instantly in a heap on the floor or on a nearby pew. Others staggered but remained standing. Pastor Kilpatrick, who had never seen anything like this happen in his church before, followed Hill on his rounds, watching and praying, his stoic face etched with a mixture of anticipation and confusion.

Rediscovering the Lost Fire

It is easy to understand his plight. As one of the Assemblies of God's leading pastors, Kilpatrick and others like him had made their churches big, successful, and dependable by largely turning their backs on their denomination's rough-and-tumble origins in the Azusa Street revivals of 1906–1909, which launched the modern pentecostal movement and many denominations, including their own.

Once populated primarily by the poor and the oppressed, who looked to church as a haven in a heartless world, Assemblies congregations had gone upscale in recent decades. As its members had moved from the periphery of American society, the denomination had become part of the American establishment. In the process, the denomination had gone mainstream. By the late 1980s and early 1990s, its decades of impressive growth had plateaued. And even though churches in the denomination still stressed being baptized in the Spirit—a postconversion experience believed to give believers a deeper experience of the fullness of God—their worship services had gradually become less chaotic and more conventional in character. Sawdust and cinder blocks had been replaced by beautiful sanctuaries decorated with plush carpet and glistening marble, like the one at Brownsville. Sunday services at most of the denomination's churches had become predictably humdrum rather than the Holy Ghost happenings that gave the movement its character.

As church historian Timothy Weber points out, the evolution of the Assemblies into a mainstream American denomination has occurred at the expense of the denomination's historic and distinctive spiritual tradition. "After all," says Weber, "if you wear a seven-hundred-fifty-dollar suit to church, you don't necessarily want to get it dirty by rolling in the aisles."

For Kilpatrick and others at Brownsville Assembly of God, all this was about to change suddenly and dramatically.

There are times on "The Father's Day Outpouring" video when Kilpatrick cannot be seen. Instead, he is just out of range as the cameras focus on Hill, who is busily praying with parishioners, increasing numbers of whom are falling to the floor.

When Kilpatrick does appear in the frame again for a moment, he looks somewhat unsteady on his feet. Then he grabs the pulpit microphone and begins to speak, sounding slightly giddy and disoriented. "The power in this place . . ." he says, his voice trailing off. "I never felt like this in my life. I feel numb."

For another few seconds the cameras leave Kilpatrick, focusing on the flurry of activity surrounding Hill. But when they come back to Kilpatrick, he is teetering on the steps in front of the pulpit. And then it happens: all the strength seems to leave his six-foot-two frame, and he goes down, tumbling onto his back next to the pulpit, his long legs hanging over the altar steps, his arms splayed back over his head, and his tie and jacket in a disheveled mess. Kilpatrick stayed on his back for the next four hours.

Although some church members filtered out of the sanctuary, many stayed for the next four hours too. During that time many were slain in the Spirit. Meanwhile, their reservations for Father's Day lunches went unfilled. And the men's carnations either wilted from the heat or were crushed under the fall of bodies.

But as Kilpatrick was soon to find out, this wild and frenzied marathon service was merely the precursor of much more to come. The Father's Day Outpouring was about to become the first chapter of a years-long event that has been hailed by believers worldwide as the Pensacola Outpouring. Kilpatrick would recall later, "As I walked across this platform, I had no idea my life and the life of this church would change so radically."

Changing Course

Many of the members of the Brownsville church did experience the fire of heaven that Father's Day, and soon talk about what had happened began spreading through the congregation. Those who weren't there could not believe their pastor had been laid out on the floor for hours, but they knew something unusual must have happened for him to cancel the Sunday evening service and schedule revival meetings with evangelist Hill beginning Monday night. Still, many did not know what to make of their conservative pastor's first dramatic steps away from order and tradition.

As for Hill, he had planned to leave Pensacola on Monday morning. The pages from his 1995 appointment book show he was due in Mobile, Alabama, on Monday night before flying to Tallahassee the following weekend. Then it was off to eastern Europe for a two-week preaching campaign in Minsk, followed by rallies in Iowa, Czechoslovakia, and other locations during the summer and fall.

But both Hill and Kilpatrick sensed that God was up to something in Pensacola and felt they must respond. "The opportunity of a lifetime must be seized during the lifetime of the opportunity," says Hill, quoting a lesson learned from his mentor, the late Leonard Ravenhill. Hill began canceling his other engagements, at first a day or two at a time, then a week or two at a time, and then, as things at Brownsville began to take off, months at a time.

Meanwhile, Kilpatrick was busy rethinking everything he ever knew about how to pastor a church. Brownsville had long been a congregation that had prayed for revival in a denomination that was formed out of revival; Kilpatrick now found himself at the helm of a congregation that was itself immersed in revival.

Kilpatrick worked to steer his congregation away from business-as-usual. From his perspective, he was leading his church into a new sensitivity and openness to the leading of the Holy Spirit. But that is not the way all the church members saw it. Although a majority embraced the revival, many never did. Dozens left within the first few months.

Others remained for much longer, suppressing their doubts and trying to go along with the new program. Among these were

Mike and Vicky Conroy, who had been members of Brownsville for more than a decade before leaving in late 1997. The couple, both of whom worked on the prayer teams that counsel people who come forward during the revival's regular altar calls, complained that the church began to place more emphasis on people's experiences than on the truths of Scripture. Vicky even claims that the church's powerful peer pressure forced her into faking unusual manifestations, including physical jerks and twirls, which others in the church interpreted as evidence of the power of God.

Even some of Kilpatrick's own staff members were initially skeptical about the changes they saw taking place around them.

Shaken and Stirred

Richard Crisco joined the staff of Brownsville in 1992 as youth pastor. Born and raised Catholic, Crisco had accepted the Lord at an Assemblies of God church, but he had never witnessed anything like what was happening at Brownsville. And initially, he was troubled by the "manifestations" that accompanied the revival.

Crisco was not the only one. As revival services stretched on for hours, hundreds of people would jerk spasmodically or fall to the ground. Others would weep loudly or beseech Jesus with heartfelt groans and pleadings. Not everyone was this demonstrative, and many quietly knelt at the altar, while others lay on the carpet in the church's aisles, lost in private spiritual reveries for hours at a time. Still, there were enough strange goings-on to ruffle the feathers of even lifelong pentecostals. As *Time* magazine religion writer Richard Ostling would later say in a report for the PBS television program *News Hour,* "At Brownsville, extravagant physical manifestations are a nightly mass phenomenon."

"I was seeing things I had never seen before," says Crisco. "I didn't know if this was of the flesh, or what. I've got two big pet peeves. One is that people are all the time looking for shortcuts in life. The other is that people can be very fickle. When revival hit, I thought about what the impact might be on the church's youth, and I saw the potential to have a lot of shallow, emotional teenagers."

But over time, Crisco's skepticism turned to enthusiasm as he saw deep, life-changing transformation take place both in his young people and in others in the church.

"Certain individuals who were always snots or brats to work with were suddenly angels," he says. "That did it for me, because I don't care if people shake, fall, or speak in tongues. I want to see a difference in their lives. And I began to see that."

Author Hank Hanegraaff and other critics of Brownsville have highlighted the unusual manifestations that have accompanied the revival. To these critics, activities such as jerking and falling have no spiritual benefit, and instead of being signs of God's power, they are warning signals that unstable souls are being led into falsehood, fanaticism, and an elevation of subjective emotional experience over the transcendent truths of Scripture. "I don't really see Brownsville as a revival at all," Hanegraaff told me in early 1998.

Crisco and others at Brownsville disagree with that assessment, but they understand the concern. "I'm not hard on critics outside the walls of this church, because if I wasn't there, I might have been one of them myself," he says. "I know the power of suggestion can be powerful. If people see someone laying hands on people, and watch some of them fall, half of them will fall themselves. And there are times where the excitement at Brownsville is so powerful that the pastor could sneeze and hundreds of people would run to the altar. I understand the critics, but I've been here, and this is real."

Lindell Cooley, the church's charismatic and talented worship leader, was hired by Brownsville two months before revival broke out, but he was in Russia on a musical missionary tour at the time of the Father's Day Outpouring. Born into a family led by a fiery pentecostal preacher, Cooley was happy to see God moving at Brownsville, but he could not get over his own discomfort with some of the jerking and shaking.

"I cringed at some of the manifestations, and I still do," he says. "At the beginning of the revival, I was very cynical about it. But I've seen that God has used different people and things to bring different revelations of Himself to us."

Hanegraaff and others have compared Brownsville to the "laughing revival," which broke out in 1993 at the Toronto Airport Vineyard church, a comparison which, according to church historian Vinson Synan, is inaccurate and unfair for three major reasons:

- First, while the Brownsville manifestations have been rowdy, they have been no more extreme than those that have accompanied earlier American revivals, particularly the Second Great Awakening, which began in southern camp meetings. And Brownsville's manifestations are far less unusual than those at Toronto, where instances of people roaring like lions, barking like dogs, crowing like chickens, and speaking out dramatic millennial prophecies have been common.

- Second, the Assemblies of God denomination has given its blessing to the Brownsville revival, and both Kilpatrick and Hill meet regularly with denominational leaders and others in a "Covering Committee" designed to provide guidance and accountability. But Vineyard leader John Wimber, who is now deceased, was unsuccessful in persuading pastor John Arnott and other Toronto leaders to control "exotic and nonbiblical manifestations" and concentrate more on Scripture. Ultimately, Wimber was forced to expel the Toronto congregation from the Association of Vineyard Churches.

- Third, at Brownsville people often hear a harsh "turn-or-burn" message of "get right with God now or else." Consequently, that revival has led approximately two hundred thousand people to dedicate or rededicate their lives to God. At Toronto there have been more sermons about the love of God, and only nine thousand first-time conversions were recorded through 1995.

Perhaps the biggest single difference between Toronto and Brownsville is Kilpatrick's close and careful management of the atmosphere at Brownsville. "One of the greatest responsibilities I have on my shoulders is pastoring this thing," he says. As part of his ongoing effort to balance a desire to see God with a commitment to preserve order, Kilpatrick counsels revival-goers against acting out. "No one draw attention to yourself," he said over the sanctuary microphone during one particularly poignant period of spiritual power. "Nobody fracture this holy moment." At other times, when excitable or unstable worshipers go wild, ushers escort them from the room.

Leaders of Toronto, which is a relatively young northern congregation in a newer charismatic denomination, and leaders of Brownsville, which is an established southern church in a historic pentecostal denomination, respect each other for the work they believe God is doing in each place, much as two farmers might admire each other's farms when their tractors come within eyesight of each other. But rather than viewing these two revivals as joined at the hip, it might be more accurate to see them as two distinct outposts of the same revivalistic phenomenon, a phenomenon that seems to respect and work within people's differing cultures and traditions rather than obliterate them.

The Fire Spreads

At first the revival at Brownsville remained a regional event. After church members, former members, and occasional guests came and checked it out for themselves, curious believers from other local churches began visiting. The church sanctuary, which had previously seemed roomy, began to fill up with guests hungry for spiritual renewal.

Soon word spread beyond the Florida panhandle that God was doing something unusual at Brownsville. Visitors began to stream in from other states, inspired by word-of-mouth testimonies, widely circulated videotapes of services, or, in many cases, by information they had received via the Internet.

Cathy Wood, a professional photographer and member of Brownsville Assembly of God, regularly uploaded photos and updates about the progress of the revival using her America Online user name, SisterWood. A growing number of people also accessed Brownsville's own Web site, as well as numerous other sites debating alleged outbreaks of revival in Pensacola and elsewhere around the world. Over time, many people who first investigated the Brownsville revival through their computers have come to Pensacola to experience the revival for themselves. "Brownsville has been a Web site revival," says Julia Duin, a reporter who has covered religion and now writes for *The Washington Times*.

Media coverage, most of it extremely positive, followed the migration of thousands of people to Pensacola. At first it was local publications like the *Pensacola News Journal* that reported on the revival. Alice Crann, a reporter for the *News Journal*, covered the revival in its early days. A story she wrote for

Charisma appeared in that magazine's October 1995 issue, becoming the first major coverage of the revival in a national Christian magazine. *Christianity Today* sent me to Florida to report on the phenomenon in 1996.

In 1997 the revival gained widespread coverage in national newspapers like *The New York Times, Washington Post,* and *USA Today,* magazines like *Newsweek* and *Spin,* and TV shows like *20/20.* A story on the Cable Network News reported that Brownsville "has become the epicenter of the pentecostal revival movement, a booming, big-time, fire-and-brimstone-driven nightly event."

Such reports transformed the trickle of visitors into a mighty flood. As interest in the revival grew, travel agent Linda Fussell, a member of the church, added staff and phone lines to handle the influx of calls from people wanting to travel to Pensacola. Soon church members were finding it tough to get seats in their own sanctuary.

In June 1996 Kilpatrick prepared to celebrate the one-year anniversary of the original Father's Day Outpouring. In a June 10 letter to church members, he wrote, "From what we hear, people from all over the country are planning to be in services over the weekend." Along with his letter Kilpatrick enclosed a ticket, and instructions for members to come early if they wanted a seat. Members, he said, could present their tickets between 8:30 and 9:15 A.M. to guarantee a place to sit in the ten o'clock service. After 9:15, nonmembers would be admitted, and members would be left out. Church members have used tickets to get into Sunday morning worship services and weeknight revival services ever since.

Visitors do not get tickets, and many of them start lining up for evening revival services long before sunrise, baking in Pensacola's summer sun or drenching in its torrential downpours for twelve hours or more. Some church members cannot bear the thought that people who have traveled from around the country or across the globe to visit the revival won't get in. So they stay home more often than they would like, to let others have a better chance of getting seats.

By the end of 1998, more than 2.5 million people had visited Brownsville, and nearly 200,000 had signed yellow "decision cards," indicating they had either experienced conversion at the revival or rededicated their lives to God there. Thousands of those who have been touched by the revival say they now want to serve God in some form of full-time Christian ministry.

In January 1997 the Brownsville Revival School of Ministry opened its doors to help such people, beginning its inaugural classes with 120 students. When the second year of classes began, there were 98 returning students from the initial class, as well as hundreds of new students. (In January 1998 the school had 666 registered students. But by the following week, school president Michael Brown reported that the institution was now past its "666 crisis," and that there were 706 full-time students.)

Brown and others working at the center of the revival see no end in sight. Meanwhile, they try to balance their joy about things they see with humility about the revival's place in the bigger picture of God's work in the world. "We don't think this is the only thing happening, but something unique is happening here," says Brown. "We view Brownsville as part of a larger complex of revival and renewal that God is bringing around the world."

Good-Bye Sunday-Go-To-Meetin'

A lot of changes have taken place at Brownsville Assembly of God since revival broke out. Sunday-go-to-meetin' decorum has been replaced by revival radicalism. The old southern-style gospel music has been replaced by a more pop-oriented contemporary sound, which invariably brings worshipers out of the cramped pews and into the aisles where they can dance, jump, and swing their arms with abandon. The old certainties of church life, including the assumption that church would start around ten on Sunday morning and end around noon—just in time for lunch—has been replaced by a packed schedule of conferences, lectures, intercessory prayer meetings, and marathon revival meetings. And the picture church members once had of themselves as a big but close-knit Christian family has been replaced by a bigger, more riotous picture featuring members as spiritual godparents to thousands of new or renewed Christian believers.

Frankly, many Brownsville members have found aspects of the revival disconcerting and disorienting. And those who have pitched in to help deal with the press of two million visitors find much of it downright wearying. There are times when some of these revival veterans wonder if it's all worth it. But then they attend one of the revival's Friday services, and afterward, everything is OK once again.

On Friday evenings, a dozen or more people who had been invited, dragged, or came to the revival and met God there in a powerful way are baptized in the baptistry located right behind the pulpit. Before they go under the water, all give a brief testimony about how God has changed their lives.

"He's done so much for me, it's time I do something for Him," said one young man during a 1998 baptismal service. Then he closed his eyes and let a volunteer lower him into the water.

Next, a young woman who is shaking so hard she can barely speak describes how she grew increasingly tired of the two people she once was: by day she was a nice church kid; but by night she was a pleasure addict who lost herself in sessions of pornography-enhanced masturbation. "I played games, went to church, and got into leadership, but it was a waste of time," she says between her sobs. "I wasted my time. I wasted God's time. I wasted a lot of people's time. I don't want to waste any more time."

Patricia from Ohio told of the wrenching emotional pain she suffered when her husband left her and her two children. "My insides were ripped to pieces," she says. "Then my mother and sister paid to have me come to this revival. God took away all my hurt. I love Him so much. He's better than any husband." As she is laid back into the pool, Patricia loses her strength and falls into the water, where she is fished out by two volunteers who carry her, limp as a dishrag, out of the baptismal area.

Doris looked straight at the congregation and explained how her once-shallow Christian commitment had not made any real difference in her life. "I accepted Jesus as my Savior and it ended there," she said. "He didn't have any part in my daily life. But now I love Him so much." Then turning from the congregation and looking heavenward, she raised her arms above her head and said: "I'm here to serve You. I'll go where You send me and say what You tell me to."

Lloyd, a forty-five-year-old pastor, said he was so burned out by ministry that he "got on a bus with nearly fifty people I didn't know in an effort to find God." Once at Brownsville, he gave God a choice: "Kill me or fill me." Then, with tears streaming down his face, he shouted: "He didn't kill me. Preachers, revival is for us."

And finally, Jack, a buzz-headed Gen-Xer said, "Till a week ago I used to be an atheist who didn't believe in God. Now that I found Him, all I want to do is be with Him."

Five years ago, members of Brownsville Assembly of God came to church and sat next to friends they had known for years. Today they never know who will be sitting in the pews. Men in suits sit next to teenage girls in baggy jeans who sit next to guys with bushy beards and tattoos who sit next to women in high heels and miniskirts. Good Christian people sit next to recovering alcoholics, former strippers, humbled businessmen, and every possible expression of the human condition.

Stinking, sin-saturated souls sit right next to sanctified saints. And for the members of Brownsville Assembly of God, that's just fine with them.

As we will see in the next chapter, such out-of-the-ordinary occurrences have been a hallmark of revival for centuries.

Changed Lives

New hope for the down-and-out

Brownsville member Ken Landon (left) has worked to redeem many men like Rob Johnson at the New Hope Home.

Down, but Not Out

If you want to talk about hard-luck stories, broken dreams, and wasted lives, these three guys have been there.

Vernon Wilkinson, who is thirty-four years old, was the tenth child of an abusive, alcoholic father and grew up in a shack home in Enterprise, Alabama, with "no lights, no water, and sometimes no food." But there was plenty of violence to go around for the kids and their mom. Once, Vernon remembers, his dad beat his mom over the head with a brick.

Life did not give Vernon many opportunities for love or success, but he frittered away the few opportunities he did have, beating every woman who ever got close to him, and losing a football scholarship to the University of Alabama after his wild partying caused a car wreck that nearly took his life. "I didn't have love as a child," says Vernon, "and the hurt, pain, and scars within me made me an extremely violent and compulsive man."

By contrast, Rob Johnson, thirty-three, grew up in a godly, loving family in Pensacola. But his mother died when he was nine, and his father, who had turned to the church to help raise his five children, never knew that a pastor had repeatedly raped Rob during his teen years. "I couldn't believe this could happen from a man in the pulpit roaring the Word of God," says Rob, who slipped into a lifestyle of cocaine addiction, anonymous gay sex, and despair.

Twenty-one-year-old Mike Combs's dad was a Hell's Angel, a pistol-packing drug dealer who was as rough with his wife as he was with guys who tried to rip him off. Drugs and alcohol were a constant in Mike's life from his earliest days. "They would get me high and get me drunk," he says. "That's how they got me to sleep at night." When Mike was eight, his dad left for good, and Mike never forgave his mom for it. He channeled his negative energy into drugs, cults, and Satanism, his all-consuming anger leading him to plot the death of his mom and a man who had sex with his girlfriend—plots that never came to pass because Mike was arrested and jailed for aggravated stalking.

Today Vernon, Rob, and Mike sit together and look back on these hair-raising stories with a mixture of sadness and joy. All three say they have been transformed by God at the Brownsville revival, and that they wouldn't have had it any other way.

"I'm glad God brought me through what He brought me

through," says Mike, "because it just gives me a greater testimony."

All three men say they would not have made it without the tough love of Ken Landon, a member of Brownsville Assembly of God and a minister–counselor at New Hope Home, a Christian alcohol and drug rehabilitation program located in nearby Gulf Breeze. Landon, who says he grew up "hating niggers, gays, hippies, and people with tattoos," wound up in prison himself for a while. That, combined with his own spiritual awakening through the Brownsville revival, led him to devote his life to serving the same kinds of people he formerly despised.

New Hope, a privately funded Christian ministry, is equal parts Bible academy, boot camp, and rehabilitation center for the thirty men who call it home. Some have been sent there by judges as an alternative to jail. Others arrived there after drugs and alcohol had ruined their lives. Vernon, Rob, Mike, and the other men at New Hope are all required to follow a rigorous, regimented schedule that includes daily Bible studies and chapel services, intensive counseling sessions, work therapy, and regular attendance at Sunday and midweek church services.

The men are also required to get involved in a local church. Vernon and Rob attend Brownsville revival services on Friday nights with Landon, and they say the grace and healing they have received there has been an essential part of their slow and gradual resurrections.

"I feel total love there, and great conviction," says Vernon.

Rob agrees. "There are people there who have been homeless and on drugs. There are people there who have walked that road. They can relate, and they can reach out further."

Mike, who once went through a short-lived jailhouse conversion, says things were different when he emerged from the baptismal at Brownsville. "God took away every bit of doubt, worry, and aggravation," he says.

The road ahead is not going to be easy for these three men. But the future probably cannot be any tougher than the past.

"There's nothing God can't do," says Rob, who has been clean and straight for two years. "Am I a new man? I didn't say I was; my family said I was. It's like night and day. I'm no longer the old man I was, with all that sin and shame."

Tears of repentance frequently flow at Brownsville, which is just the latest chapter in a centuries-old story of renewal and revival.

CHAPTER THREE

The Heartbeat of the Church:

Revival in Christian History

On October 4, 1997, hundreds of thousands of men gathered at the Mall in Washington, D.C., for Stand in the Gap: A Sacred Assembly of Men, the biggest and boldest event in the unique history of a group called Promise Keepers.

"The goal of Stand in the Gap is to gather a diverse multitude of men to confess personal and collective sin," said Promise Keepers founder Bill McCartney. "We hope to present to the Lord men on their knees in humility, then on their feet in unity, reconciled and posed for spiritual awakening."

The daylong rally, which was three years in the planning and budgeted at ten million dollars, was managed by Dale Schlafer, a Promise Keepers executive whose title—Vice President for Revival and Spiritual Awakening—says much about the event's intended purpose.

"In both the Old Testament and the New Testament, we see cycles of revival," said Schlafer. "We're in a pre-revival state with little pockets springing up, but it's not full-blown revival yet. If we would confess our sin and repent, perhaps God would ignite the church to be what He wants it to be."

A month after the men who had gathered in the nation's capital returned to their homes, their families, and their jobs, Campus Crusade for Christ founder Bill Bright hosted Fasting and Prayer

'97, one of a number of efforts the evangelical leader had organized to hasten revival in America.

Like Stand in the Gap, Fasting and Prayer '97 emphasized the need for believers to humble themselves before God. "God blesses or judges countries and cultures according to the obedience or disobedience of His children," said Bright, whose book *The Coming Revival* is an urgent plea for believers to get serious about God's desire to bless His followers.

Bright's three-day event brought thousands of Christian pastors and leaders together in Dallas for a period of fasting, prayer, and unity. The event was designed as a prelude to a forty-day period of prayer and fasting for American believers in March and April 1998.

"There has never been a greater need in all of history for Christians to fast, pray, repent, and seek the face of God," said Bright. "We're asking God to send revival to our nation and the world to enable us to help fulfill the Great Commission."

Stand in the Gap and Fasting and Prayer '97 are only two of the more highly publicized contemporary efforts to pray for and promote revival in America and around the world. The shelves at Christian bookstores are heavy with books on the subject. Churches and conference centers offer workshops on how to pray and prepare for God to awaken His people. Untold numbers of individuals, churches, and ministry organizations are committing to regular prayer times for global renewal. As the world rushes toward the end of the second millennium after Christ, millions of believers seem to be uniting behind the sentiments of the old hymn:

Revive us again;
Fill each heart with Thy love,
May each soul be rekindled
With fire from above.

This growing interest in revival is, many believe, a good and even necessary thing, for revival is at the heart—not the periphery—of the history of the faith. In his 1845 introduction to Banner of Truth's hefty "Historical Collections of Accounts of Revival," editor Horatius Bonar writes,

> Indeed, such narratives as those with which this work abounds form the true history of the Church . . . To see how God has been working, and to mark the means by which he has carried on his work, cannot fail to be profitable and quickening.

Stewards of the Commission

Jesus' disciples may not have known it when they first agreed to follow Him, but they were in for quite a ride. They followed their teacher as He spoke to the adoring crowds, and they were with Him when He eluded the screaming lynch mobs. They endured the horror of the crucifixion and celebrated the miracle of the resurrection. At each step along the way, they got a clearer picture of who Jesus was and what His life really meant.

Then, as the resurrected Christ prepared to ascend to His heavenly Father, He gave the disciples their final assignment. "Go into all the world and preach the gospel to every creature," he says at the end of the gospel of Mark. The same assignment, which believers through the centuries have called the Great Commission, is stated in a slightly different form at the end of Matthew.

And it appears once again in the opening chapter of the book of Acts. But this time the commission is coupled with a promise that God will give the disciples the spiritual vitality they need to carry out such a herculean task: "But you shall receive power when the Holy Spirit has come upon you; and you shall be witnesses to Me in Jerusalem, and in all Judea and Samaria, and to the end of the earth" (1:8).

That promise was fulfilled on the day of pentecost, when the house in which the believers had huddled was invaded by a mighty wind, and these once-confused disciples were touched by tongues of fire. Next, these first Christians were acting like worshipers at a pentecostal revival meeting: speaking in tongues and carrying on so much that casual observers assumed that "they are full of new wine" (Acts 2:13).

The remainder of the book of Acts reports on the amazing deeds of these empowered and emboldened believers. They preached the gospel, and thousands of hearers converted. They formed a close, communal bond that modern cult-watchers would certainly condemn as the worst form of spiritual abuse—pooling their possessions, devoting themselves to their leaders' teaching, and doing little else but proclaiming and promoting the kingdom of God. At every step, their efforts were punctuated with dramatic healings and miracles.

By the end of the book of Acts, missionary journeys had carried the gospel message to much of the known world, and Paul, one of the faith's most aggressive evangelists, could confidently claim: "The salvation of God has been sent to the Gentiles, and they will hear it!" (Acts 28:28).

So much for the honeymoon.

Paul's letters to the churches he founded reveal that within a few short decades, the fires of pentecost had significantly cooled. Believers had to be reminded not to sue, slander, or sleep with each other. Those who refused to submit to discipline were booted out. Divisions and heresies crept in. Suddenly, fulfilling Christ's Great Commission—or even living out a vital Christian faith—did not look so easy.

The final book of the New Testament, John's otherworldly Revelation, shows how far things had gone. In seven urgent messages to churches located in the Roman province of Asia, Jesus described the good things and the bad things He saw in these important congregations. Beginning with the church of Ephesus, a body of believers Paul had founded and praised for its growth in grace, Jesus praised their perseverance amid persecution. But then He chided them for their spiritual slackness:

Nevertheless I have this against you, that you have left your first love. Remember therefore from where you have fallen; repent and do the first works, or else I will come to you quickly and remove your lampstand from its place— unless you repent. (2:4–5)

Likewise, Jesus lashed out at the church of Sardis: "I know your works, that you have a name that you are alive, but you are dead" (3:1). And He delivered a particularly brutal criticism of the church of Laodicea:

I know your works, that you are neither cold nor hot. I could wish you were cold or hot. So then, because you are lukewarm, and neither cold nor hot, I will vomit you out of My mouth. Because you say, "I am rich, have become wealthy, and have need of nothing"—and do not know that you are wretched, miserable, poor, blind, and naked—I counsel you to buy from Me gold refined in the fire . . . Therefore be zealous and repent. (3:15–18, 19)

In less that a century, these once vibrant churches had grown lethargic and loveless. The fire, once burning brightly enough to inflame believers and enlighten converts, was growing dim. The power of pentecost was growing weak.

Reviving the Flame

This drama of fire and frost, power and impotence, has been a recurring motif in the cycles of church history for the last twenty centuries. Nothing is new under the sun, including the ongoing challenge facing believers, congregations, Christian organizations, and denominations to maintain the zeal that motivated them in the early days. Revival, wrote chronicler John Gillies in 1754, is like a refreshing rain from God that revitalizes a parched earth: "barrenness prevails and desolation covers the land. Then he opens the windows of heaven, and the swollen torrents rush along the valleys, diffusing life on every side."

Unfortunately, the New Testament does not give believers a blueprint for how revival is supposed to happen. In John's Revelation, Jesus merely told the seven churches to "repent," to "hold fast," and to "be faithful until death." This is good advice, but hardly enough upon which to construct a coherent theology of revival.

Thankfully, more detailed information about revival comes from a somewhat surprising source: the Old Testament. There the stories of Josiah, king of Judah, and Ezra and Nehemiah, restorers and reformers of Jerusalem, show that revival is a tool God has used with His people for millennia.

Reading about the deeds and misdeeds of Old Testament kings calls to mind the petty foibles and grand falls of contemporary politicians, business leaders, and evangelists. You can get a picture of how bad things had become for the Jewish people by this description of King Josiah, a man who was hailed as an outstanding good guy for adhering to a bare minimum of righteousness: "And he did what was right in the sight of the LORD, and walked in all the ways of his father David; he did not turn aside to the right hand or to the left" (2 Kings 22:2).

The important lesson we can draw from the story of Josiah's life is that revival often comes through the dedication and perseverance of one single person whose commitment to God is deep and sincere.

At the time of Josiah's reign during the sixth century B.C., Israel had already fallen because of its growing wickedness, and Judah was barely hanging on for dear life. The Pentateuch, otherwise known as the Book of the Law, had ceased to be the people's rule of life and, in fact, had disappeared altogether. When Judah's high priest rediscovered the Book and brought it to Josiah, the king recommitted himself to following its precepts, and brought his people along with him.

> *Then the king stood by a pillar and made a covenant before the LORD, to follow the LORD and to keep His commandments and His testimonies and His statutes, with all his heart and all his soul . . . And all the people took a stand for the covenant. (2 Kings 23:3)*

God honored Josiah, not only for his work to revive faith in God and reform his people, but according to the prophetess Huldah, God also honored Josiah "because your heart was tender, and you humbled yourself before the LORD when you heard what I spoke" (2 Kings 22:19).

A century later, both Israel and Judah were no more, the victims of both their spiritual infidelity and their inability to remain strong in a rapidly changing world. God's people suffered through an incredibly long and dark night of their collective soul known as the Babylonian captivity. The story of Nehemiah the governor, Ezra the priest, and the two men's concern for the welfare of Jerusalem illustrates an important point that certainly is not lost on Brownsville revival leaders John Kilpatrick and Steve Hill: God often uses two people in tandem to accomplish His aims.

Further, the work of Nehemiah and Ezra reveals that true revival is a mysterious combination of human and divine elements. Both those who claim revival is wholly divine and those who claim it can be worked up by human effort are missing the boat. Instead, it is a joint effort between God and His people.

Nehemiah successfully rebuilt Jerusalem's shattered walls, an amazing fifty-two-day feat, accomplished though the workers were constantly assailed by doubts from within and criticism from without. When it was done, even Nehemiah's enemies declared that the project's completion showed evidence of God's helping hand.

Meanwhile, Ezra's efforts to reform the people of Jerusalem spiritually were much less speedy, yet significant reform happened. Ultimately, the people recommitted themselves to a covenant with God. It's safe to say these spiritual reform efforts would have been much more difficult if the people had not had the physical security that came from Nehemiah's wall.

What Is Revival?

If Josiah, Nehemiah, and Ezra were asked to describe revival, each one would probably emphasize different aspects of the reform and renewal efforts they participated in. Likewise, contemporary revival advocates like Bill McCartney, Bill Bright, and the leaders of the Brownsville revival have slightly different ideas about precisely what God is doing today.

Scholars and historians who have struggled to come up with a definition of revival have not done much better in arriving at a consensus. But as they have examined the numerous revival movements that have helped revitalize the church over the last twenty centuries, they have agreed on some of the big concepts. Take a look at some of the following efforts to define revival, and see which one makes the most sense to you.

- Zondervan's *New International Dictionary of the Christian Church* describes revival as:

  > A spontaneous spiritual awakening by the Holy Spirit among professing Christians in the churches, which results in deepened religious experience, holy living, evangelism and missions, the founding of educational and philanthropic institutions, and social reform.

- Or here's how IVP's *Dictionary of Christianity in America* puts it:

  > Revivalism is the movement that promotes periodic spiritual intensity in church life, during which the unconverted come to Christ and the converted are shaken out of their spiritual lethargy.

- And Baker's *Evangelical Dictionary of Theology* describes revivalism as:

  > A movement within the Christian tradition which emphasizes the appeal of religion to the emotional and affectional nature of individuals as well as to their intellectual and rational nature. It believes that vital Christianity begins with a response of the whole being to the gospel's call for repentance and spiritual rebirth by faith in Jesus Christ. This experience results in a personal relationship with God.

Instead of trying to find a perfect definition, perhaps it would be more beneficial to focus on some of the major characteristics that have been most prominent in revivals throughout history. Among the many characteristics, the following ten have been the most important.

1. Saints are revived. Revival often begins with believers, transforming once lethargic laypeople into zealous servants of God.

2. Sinners are saved. During revival, classic sinners such as prostitutes and drunks join society's beautiful people at the altar to confess their evil ways and seek God's forgiveness.

3. Sermons hit home. Eerdman's *Handbook to Christianity in America* says that one of the major characteristics of America's Second Great Awakening was "simple, lively, and persuasive preaching." Revival sermons shy away from complex theology to focus on the basic gospel message of sin and salvation in its staggering simplicity, often upping the ante with descriptive pictures of the sufferings of hell.

4. Music moves the masses. Whether it was the tag team of brothers John and Charles Wesley or the collaboration of evangelist Dwight L. Moody and song leader Ira Sankey, musicians have augmented the impact of revival sermons by stirring people's emotions and helping them sing their praises to God.

5. Churches work together. When revival hits, workers seize the opportunity without worrying about preserving strict denominational purity.

6. People do strange things. Evangelical etiquette usually dictates that believers keep a lid on their emotions. But during revival, people overcome with a sense of the closeness of God lose control and often begin weeping, wailing, falling, jerking, screaming "Hallelujah," or experiencing an outpouring of spiritual gifts. Revival, at least for the past few centuries, has been a rowdy, messy affair.

7. Believers battle sin. Billy Sunday attacked demon rum. Charles Finney went after Christians who smoked. And sexual sins have always been seen as a satanic stronghold. Today Brownsville evangelist Steve Hill warns of the dangers of online pornography, showing that times change, but the fundamental battle doesn't.

8. Society is influenced. Born-again believers have founded schools, universities, and Bible colleges; fought evils like slavery and child labor; and campaigned to elect godly leaders to office, showing that while revival may begin as an individual awakening, it ultimately has an impact on the culture beyond the doors of the church.

9. Missions and evangelism flourish. Revival transformed William Booth, who went on to found the Salvation Army, now one of the world's largest Christian organizations. Likewise, revival sparked many of the world's biggest and best-known missionary groups, evangelism efforts, parachurch organizations, and Christian denominations.

10. Controversy causes clashes. Brownsville is not the first revival to stir up arguments. Christians look back with dewy-eyed affection at the first Great Awakening, which had a powerful effect on pre-Revolutionary America. But at the time, prominent Boston minister Charles Chauncy ascribed the whole affair to mental illness. Revival has always been a divisive force.

Different Ways to Wake the Dead

Our ideas about what constitutes revival have been greatly influenced by events that have happened on American soil over the past three and one-half centuries. But long before there was a Christian presence in America, God was finding creative ways to shake things up in other parts of the world. Here is a brief look at four unique periods of awakening, each of which reveals the diverse ways in which spiritual entropy can be overcome.

Devotion in the Desert

By the early fourth century, Christianity was well on its way to becoming the official religion of the Roman Empire. Many welcomed the relief from centuries of persecution that such official status would bring, but others saw the growing embrace of the Empire as the prelude to a death grip that would wring the spiritual life out of the church.

Antony of Egypt fled civilization to seek silence and solitude in the deserts near the Dead Sea, where he spent hours at a time praying to God and battling the devil. But soon Antony's solitude was interrupted by the arrival of a few—and then hundreds—of followers who wanted to learn from this rugged holy man. Antony organized his fellow hermits into groups, forming the Christian faith's first monastic communities. Along with his fellow monks, Antony not only rekindled the communal *koinonia* of the first-century church, but he endowed the evolving Christian tradition with a depth of sanctity and devotion that would serve as a powerful antidote to the watered-down, state-sanctioned faith.

Monks as Missionaries

Antony's harsh asceticism was embraced by Ireland's Celtic Christian converts, who established monasteries on the tops of high hills where pagan rites had once been practiced and on inaccessible islands where they could be alone with God and creation.

Many Celtic monks, such as the sixth century's Brendan the Voyager, combined a love for home with an unquenchable zeal to sail off to distant lands. Some even went into their boats, took down their sails, and let God guide them across the wild waves. Their travels took the Celtic monks throughout much of the known—and parts of the unknown—world. They preached the gospel and set up monasteries in England, Scotland, France, Germany, Austria, Switzerland, and Italy. These monks also had an insatiable love of learning, leading them to study and copy ancient manuscripts, both Christian and otherwise. After the Roman Empire fell, Celtic monasteries became the repositories of some of the Western world's most prized literary traditions.

Following a Follower of Jesus

One of the people who visited the Italian monastery at Bobbio, which the Celtic monks had founded, was the thirteenth-century Saint Francis of Assisi. Following a dramatic vision in which God told him to rebuild His church, Francis abandoned his wealthy family and his worldly goods and began repairing a neglected, rundown sanctuary.

Soon Francis's radical simplicity, deep devotion to Jesus, and compassion for all God's creatures attracted followers. His obedience to biblical teachings on poverty and humility provided a sharp contrast to the growing wealth and power of the Roman Catholic church. He preached to birds, but he also preached to Muslims—a radical move during the time of the Crusades, when the standard approach to conversion used swords, not words. By the time of his death, Francis had thousands of followers. Today there are a million Franciscans around the world, making them the largest order in the Catholic church.

Radical Reformers

Francis's life and message curbed some of the worst excesses of the Catholic church, but a growing group of reformers believed more radical reform was needed. Dominican priest Savonarola preached against papal power and corruption before being hanged and burned in a plaza in Florence in 1498. English Bible translator William Tyndale began printing his New Testaments in 1525, an act that led to his being continually harassed and hounded before being strangled and burned eleven years later.

In 1517 Augustinian priest Martin Luther issued his Ninety-five Theses, which attacked not only the scandalous sale of indulgences but the entire Roman church. Charged with heresy, he refused to recant, hiding out in Germany, where he continued his writing and teaching. Those who came after Luther, including Zwingli, Calvin, and Knox, helped permanently transform the Christian faith.

Revival American-Style

American revivalism got its beginning with a decades-long series of renewals historians call the Great Awakening. America was not even a nation when revival started in 1725, and when the Awakening calmed down around 1760, it was clear that the fiery rhetoric of evangelists like George Whitefield would leave a lasting legacy.

Whitefield was only twenty-four when he came to preach in the American colonies in 1740. He was already famous in his native England, where the piety of the Wesleys would radically change his life. Ordained in the Church of England, Whitefield developed a unique form of preaching that bore no resemblance to the lofty oratory of other Anglican clerics. He proclaimed a simple and direct message that could be understood by the commoner as well as the cultured. And instead of preaching from pulpits and relying on copious notes, Whitefield took his messages to the people, preaching extemporaneous, biblically based sermons on farms and in fields, depending on God to give him the words he needed to say. Throngs turned out to hear the man who is now regarded by many historians as the father of modern evangelicalism.

American ministers like Jonathan Edwards had paved the way for Whitefield with their own powerful preaching. Edwards, widely regarded as the keenest theologian our country has ever produced, proclaimed a straightforward message in sermons like his famous "Sinners in the Hands of an Angry God." When Edwards and others invited Whitefield to preach up and down the eastern seaboard, small, localized pockets of renewal erupted into a widespread revival. Historian Richard Bushman writes that the impact was "like the civil rights demonstrations, the campus disturbances, and the urban riots of the 1960s combined."

Whitefield aimed some of his strongest verbal barrages at lukewarm pastors. As he wrote in his journals:

The Lord enabled me to open my mouth boldly against unconverted ministers . . . For I am verily persuaded the generality of preachers talk of an unknown and unfelt Christ; and the reasons why congregations have been so dead is, because they have dead men preaching to them . . . For how can dead men beget living children?

Not surprisingly, some colonial ministers did not appreciate Whitefield's pointed barbs. Others disliked the revival's unbridled emotionalism and populist appeal. But American revivalism would only become wilder and more controversial during the outbreak known as the Second Great Awakening.

As with the earlier revival, this later period of spiritual renewal was characterized by varied regional renewal movements covering a number of decades, beginning in the 1780s and continuing through the 1820s. But it was a series of outdoor camp meetings held in Kentucky between 1800 and 1801 that gave this awakening its distinctive character and unique place in history.

As many as twenty thousand people attended the six-day camp meeting organized by Barton Stone and local Presbyterians and Methodists in 1801 at Cane Ridge, Kentucky. This was raw religion for a rugged, frontier people, and in addition to mass conversions there were mass convulsions. People shook, jerked, and fell to the ground.

As important as these powerful periods of revival were, there is one person who has probably had a greater impact on how Americans understand revivalism today. That man, Charles Finney, was so turned off by some of the excesses of the Second Great Awakening that he deemed them "spurious." Still, historians now refer to him as the father of modern revivalism.

An attorney who was converted in 1821 and later ordained as a Presbyterian pastor, Finney described himself as someone on "a retainer from the Lord to plead His cause." As we will see in the next chapter, Finney developed a series of "New Measures" designed to help believers streamline the process of revival. These measures, though controversial, have had a profound impact on the direction and shape of nineteenth and twentieth century revival and evangelism efforts.

New Things from the Lord

When historians look back on the twentieth century, will they label it America's Third Great Awakening? It's too early to tell. But one thing is already clear: the Azusa Street revival, which erupted in the early years of this century, has had a profound, long-term, and worldwide impact on the history of the faith.

Azusa Street is in Los Angeles, but some say the revival that occurred there really began far away in Wales, where a young man named Evan Roberts prayed and pleaded with God to bring refreshing to his country. The impact of the Welsh revival of 1904–1906 spread around the globe, touching many churches in America.

As things were winding down in Wales, William Seymour, an African-American evangelist, felt God calling him to Los Angeles. He assumed God would lead him to a church. Instead, Seymour wound up at a small Los Angeles house where he and other believers met together for periods of prayer. On April 9, 1906, that humble house was the site of a second pentecost. Seymour and those with him began speaking in tongues. Soon so many people were turning up at the house to receive this spiritual gift that a new location had to be found. A warehouse at 312 Azusa Street fit the bill.

The Azusa Street revival continued for another three years, gaining plenty of attention in *The Los Angeles Times*. One story described how "the devotees of the weird doctrine practice the most fanatical rites, preach the wildest theories, and work themselves into a state of mad excitement in their peculiar zeal."

That zeal resulted in a powerful renewal that spread to other states. In addition, many of the people who were renewed at Azusa Street went out to spread the pentecostal message far and wide. The revival also had a powerful effect on the Christian and Missionary Alliance denomination, and it led to the founding of a number of new pentecostal denominations, including the Assemblies of God, which was formed in 1914.

From these humble beginnings, pentecostalism has swept around the globe. Today, according to historian Vinson Synan, pentecostals worldwide make up the largest group of Christians after Catholics, and they are the largest group within Protestantism.

Some observers also say other twentieth-century movements qualify as revivals.

The Healing Revival

According to historian David Edwin Harrell, this outbreak, which ran from 1947 to 1958, was inspired by Charles Parham (who before his death in 1929 had been a teacher of Azusa Street's William Seymour) and promoted by the tireless preaching of Oral Roberts. These and other healing evangelists traveled around the country preaching in large tent revivals, promising that God would heal their hearers' physical ailments. Although many believers swore by their cures, it was hard to convince skeptical journalists and critical denominational leaders of the revival's benefits.

The Charismatic Renewal

A diverse group of leaders helped propel this 1960s movement, including Demos Shakarian, founder of the Full Gospel Business Men's Fellowship; Episcopalian priest Dennis Bennett; and Assemblies of God preacher and street minister David Wilkerson. By the 1970s there were charismatic prayer groups operating either clandestinely or with full permission in most major Protestant denominations, and a major Catholic charismatic movement was gathering steam. The charismatic renewal brought millions of nonpentecostal believers a renewed sense of personal and corporate worship, allowing them to experience more of the fullness of God without leaving their own churches and traditions.

The Jesus Movement

During the 1960s American young people were experimenting with mind-expanding drugs, revolutionary ideologies, and Eastern religions—anything, in fact, but homegrown Christianity, which was rejected as phony and plastic. But at Christian coffeehouses, contemporary Christian music concerts, and churches like Chuck Smith's Calvary Chapel in southern California, spiritually hungry youth were confronted with the radical and life-changing message of Jesus. Today, the rock/pop-style music, no-nonsense messages, and relaxed worship style that characterized the first Jesus people are staples at many evangelical churches.

If the apostle John were to deliver an updated version of his Revelation to the contemporary churches of America, there would be plenty to praise as well as much to criticize.

Many churches are making efforts to awaken and renew believers, and to return them to their first love. At Brownsville Assembly of God, such efforts began with Pastor John Kilpatrick and the prayers of a congregation.

Changed Lives

From dry to dynamic

Mike and Lorraine Brown (center) were longtime Brownsville members who saw their lives, and those of sons Justin (left) and Joshua (right), radically changed.

Revival, Family Style

Lorraine Brown's connections to the Brownsville Assembly of God go way back. Her parents, along with an aunt and an uncle, were among the church's founders, attending religiously from day one. Growing up, Lorraine attended Sunday school at

Brownsville, and in 1970 she married her husband, Michael, there. (He is not related to Brownsville Revival School of Ministry president Michael L. Brown.)

In 1995, after attending the Assemblies' Bible school in Springfield, Missouri, and pastoring a number of churches, Michael and Lorraine returned to Brownsville with their three children.

Lorraine loved Brownsville, believing it to be a solid and spiritually dynamic church. But by 1995 she felt her own personal spiritual life was more a matter of ritual than renewal. "For some reason, I had a dryness in my relationship with the Lord," she says. "I couldn't understand it, because I was trying to do what a good Christian should do."

Things changed dramatically after Father's Day 1995, when Brownsville was hit by the revival that spread throughout the congregation and deeply touched the entire Brown family.

Lorraine and Michael were the first to receive a fresh blessing from God. Suddenly, spiritual dryness was replaced by rivers of joy. "People came forward for prayer and would fall out in the Spirit, dancing and jerking," says Lorraine. "That was not usual for me. I knew something was different."

Next, their daughter, Jennifer, experienced a spiritual awakening; she later married a man in the church's worship team.

Son Joshua, who was fourteen years old when revival broke out, could not help but notice the difference in his parents, and particularly his sister. "I saw a real change in her," he says.

The only changes Joshua had seen in himself in recent years were bad ones. He says he had been a strong Christian until he hit seventh grade. "I was trying to witness to people who had a stronger influence on me than I had on them," he says. He began experimenting with drugs, dabbling in the occult, becoming depressed, and considering suicide. Along the way he grew rebellious. "I got harder. I had fights with my parents. I let them know I hated them."

When he went off to summer camp in 1996, Josh thought hard about his life. "I had built a wall between me and God. I knew I had to serve Jesus or serve Satan, and all Satan ever gave me was anger and bitterness. I knew my friends would diss me, but I gave my life to God and talked to Him as a friend." Now Josh says he plans to enter the ministry.

Justin, who at age eleven was the youngest child in the family, had seen the changes in his parents and his sister, but the transformation in Josh had an impact on him. "I thought I was saved before," says Justin. "I thought God was OK. But I was getting harder myself. The change in Josh's life eventually brought me along."

Lorraine looks at her sons and says, "If it weren't for the revival . . ."

But her voice trails off as she thinks about all the could-have-beens, of all the destructive paths her children could have taken. "I'm just real thankful," she says.

Today Lorraine expresses joy for everything God has done for her, her church, and her family by singing in Brownsville's 146-voice adult choir. Like everything else at Brownsville, the choir has been transformed by revival (and, Lorraine adds, by the arrival of worship leader Lindell Cooley two months before revival broke out). Choir members still wear robes, but now they sing, dance, and weep with an unbridled joy. That's not the way things used to be.

"We were basically a conservative white choir with a limited repertoire," she says. "But now it's getting to where we all really enjoy the Lord. There's a lot more freedom of expression."

PART II

Movers and Shakers

Brownsville's John Kilpatrick had prayed for revival, but no one knew it would happen like it has.

CHAPTER FOUR

Prepare Ye the Way:

Pastor John Kilpatrick

For those who have long been familiar with Brownsville Assembly of God, the most amazing thing about the revival there is not that millions of people have visited, or that hundreds of thousands have made commitments for Christ, or that revival has continued for more than three years.

Rather, for those who know Brownsville and its pastor, John Kilpatrick, the most amazing thing of all was that *this* kind of revival happened in *this* church and under *this* man.

"Knowing me, a lot of people came to see what was happening here," says forty-seven-year-old Kilpatrick. "That's one of the biggest reasons this revival gained a lot of attention."

Even Kilpatrick himself is somewhat surprised that revival broke out at Brownsville. "Each night as I walk into our sanctuary, my emotions are overwhelmed and my mind is boggled. At times, this really doesn't feel like this is happening to us. It feels like it is happening at someone else's church, and I'm just a spectator.

"I only know that God has visited us. There is an open heaven above this place."

Kilpatrick is quick to point out that there's no such thing as a surefire, easy-to-follow, five-step method for bringing revival to a church. And he readily admits that the awakening that began in his congregation in 1995 may end tomorrow, and there's absolutely nothing he can do about it. Still, there are lessons one can learn from the life of this now-famous pastor, lessons that show how God can use a life that is yielded and committed.

Flawed Family Values

Kilpatrick often preaches about biblical teachings on the family. Husbands and wives should love and cherish each other. Moms and dads are to care for their children and guide them in the ways of the Lord. Children who honor their parents will be blessed by God all the days of their lives.

The family Kilpatrick was born into could not be farther from this rosy picture. His mother, Era Mae, was a dark-skinned woman of Native American descent with a sixth-grade education; she was unlucky enough to be the fifth of seven wives of J. C. Kilpatrick, a man whose weakness for women and angry tirades made him an ineffectual husband and father.

Growing up in humble circumstances in the mill town of Columbus, Georgia, John Alton Kilpatrick was accustomed to his father's yelling and fighting. The younger Kilpatrick was eight years old when his father left the family for the first time, and twelve when he left for the last time.

For a while the boy was shipped off to live with his grandparents near tiny, rural Troy, Alabama. Kilpatrick remembers these times as "lonely and quiet." He had no one his age to play with, and he feared his mama might never come back for him.

It was a dark time, but it left a profound imprint on Kilpatrick's preaching. His rousing Sunday morning sermons overflow with images of nature and farm life, which he observed around his grandparents' home. This not only gives him an innate appreciation for the agrarian settings of some of Jesus' most powerful parables, but it also provides a nearly limitless repertoire of effective illustrations.

In one 1998 sermon Kilpatrick repeatedly used the image of

a scarecrow to represent things that prevent God's children from experiencing all the things their heavenly Father has for them. "If you've ever spent much time in the country," he said, "you've seen scarecrows. They're ugly, awkward, and shabby, with ghastly arms." But a scarecrow is merely an effigy, he said, and a wise blackbird does not allow himself to be scared away. "It's all right," the bird crows out to his fearful friends, who seek safety in faraway trees or power lines. "This old scarecrow won't hurt you. Come on down. There's good eating down here."

Kilpatrick even describes the revival at Brownsville in earthy, rural images. Asked about the months and years before revival broke out, he replies, "It was like a thunderstorm. You can smell it before it rains. I smelled revival before it came."

After three months in Alabama, Kilpatrick's mama rescued him, taking him back to Columbus, where she worked scrubbing floors at a nursing home and took her son to church at Eighth Street Assembly of God. Kilpatrick knew God was with him, but he still could not shake feelings of anger and dread. In a desperate effort to please his mama, he promised her he would be a preacher some day. When his father heard about this, he bluntly told the boy, "I'd rather see you dead than with a Bible under your arm."

The call to preach would come soon enough, however, but not from such a dubious source as the agitated mind of a troubled youngster. Instead, Kilpatrick's call would come directly from the voice of Almighty God.

It was a Tuesday morning and fourteen-year-old Kilpatrick was sitting in biology class at Arnold Junior High School. As he writes in his book *Feast of Fire*, he was supposed to be watching a science film, but instead he was praying for God to touch his life.

At that point, it seemed like someone reached over to the projector knob and lowered the sound . . . Just then I heard an audible voice come into my left ear and I knew it was the voice of the Lord. Why? Because He called me by my first name, John. I had always been called by my middle name, Alton. While growing up I never heard anyone refer to me as John. I just knew this was the voice of God speaking to me.

"John, this day I have called you to preach My Word," He said to me. "I want you to stay away from the other boys and girls in your neighborhood who would be a bad influence in your life. Don't go with them. If you do, I will lose you." . . .

The projector sound came right back up at that point and though I did not feel any differently, I knew God had just called me, right there in biology class watching a film on dissecting a frog.

Certain in his call, Kilpatrick turned to R. C. Wetzel, pastor of Riverview Assembly of God, who served as a strong and loving mentor and father figure. Wetzel grilled Kilpatrick in how to preach, but perhaps more importantly, he gave the youngster a living demonstration of the softness of a pastor's heart through his compassion for his flock and his earnestness in seeking God in prayer.

The Riverview congregation was also where Kilpatrick found his future wife, Brenda. At first the pretty and popular Brenda had little interest in church, and even less in marrying a preacher. But her mother had a dream in which Brenda was drinking and laughing in "smoky beer joints," and walking with a limp, which had been caused by a terrible car accident. "That's what you'll be like if you don't come to the Lord," warned her mother. Before long, Brenda had recommitted herself to Christ and married Kilpatrick.

After pastoring two small churches in the Georgia towns of Vidalia and Warner Robins, Kilpatrick accepted a call to Calvary Temple Assembly of God in the "cold country" of Evansville, Indiana. During three years there, the church grew from 650 to 1,000 members, and Kilpatrick grew from a country preacher to a seasoned, professional pastor. Now the thirty-two-year-old Kilpatrick was ready to return to the South and pastor the Brownsville Assembly of God.

From "Proper" to Prayerful

Kilpatrick arrived at Brownsville in February 1982 and threw himself into guiding the congregation with vigor and vision. Under his leadership the church began a weekly television broadcast in 1986, and built its current 2,100-seat sanctuary in 1989.

Along the way Kilpatrick developed a reputation as the tough, no-nonsense pastor of a solid, conservative congregation. Youth minister Richard Crisco recalls that prior to revival, "This church was very conservative, straight-laced, and proper; and so was its pastor." Even worship services were nothing to shout about. "Everything was slow, and decent, and in order," says Crisco.

Worship leader Lindell Cooley, who was hired on at Brownsville two months before revival broke out in 1995, hadn't been sure he wanted to work for a conventional pastor like Kilpatrick at an "IBM-type" church like Brownsville. "The church was immaculate and everything was in its proper place, just like its pastor," remembers Cooley.

Kilpatrick describes the pre-revival Brownsville as a church that was successful but dry. "The people were wonderful, we had a good name in the city, and I felt we were making our mark as much as any church," he says. "But who wants to be in 'religion'? If God is real and He can do things, let's see it."

Increasingly, Kilpatrick began to seek more from God, both for himself and for his church. "I would say, 'God, if I'm going to give my life for this thing, I want to see You work. But if there's no power, I'd rather pump gas or flip hamburgers.'"

In 1991 one of many prophecies about revival in America caught Kilpatrick's ears. The source of this prophecy was Dr. David Yonggi Cho, pastor of Yoido Full Gospel Church in Seoul, South Korea, the largest church in the world. While preaching in Seattle, Washington, Cho—who prays daily for America—became troubled by the spiritual decline of this country. After praying even more earnestly, Cho says God prompted him to get a map of the United States and point his finger where he was directed. His finger landed on Pensacola. "Then," Cho says, "I sensed the Lord say, 'I am going to send revival to the seaside city of Pensacola, and it will spread like a fire until all of America has been consumed by it.'"

This prophecy—one of many Brownsville revival supporters say paved the way for the awakening there—increased Kilpatrick's desire to see God work in all His glory. He began to talk about revival, teach about revival, and preach about revival—so much so that some church members thought he was sounding like a broken record. In a 1993 sermon entitled "The Protocol of Heaven," he said, "I believe this church is on the threshold of something big."

Kilpatrick says God reminded him of Jesus' comment in Matthew 21: "My house shall be called a house of prayer." And immediately, the church changed its long-established Sunday evening routine. Kilpatrick quit giving Sunday evening sermons, and instead, these services emphasized corporate prayer.

In order to give direction to these prayer meetings, church members designed and created twelve large banners, roughly three feet wide by six feet tall, each of which focused on a different spiritual issue. There were banners for spiritual warfare, family, souls, national leaders, healing, pastors, the peace of Jerusalem, schools, the church, and revival. Later, banners were added for children and survivors of catastrophes.

With the banners serving as towering physical symbols, church members attending the Sunday evening prayer services would write down prayer requests and place them at the base of the relevant banner. Then, during increasingly intense periods of prayer, members would kneel, stand, and walk around the banners, pleading with God as they focused on the subject depicted in the banner. Over time, more and more members began gravitating toward and praying around the revival banner.

You can hassle and harass Kilpatrick, trying to pry out of him some surefire method to bring revival down. But he refuses to play along, insisting there is nothing particularly special about him or anybody else at Brownsville. All he will say is that revival would not have happened without his congregation's steadfast and serious commitment to seeking God, beginning more than two years before revival broke out.

"Prayer always precedes a great work of God," he says.

And intense, regular prayer continues to be a Brownsville tradition. Every Tuesday night the church sponsors a prayer meeting led by Intercessory Prayer Coordinator Lila Terhune. Unlike events you may have attended that were advertised as prayer meetings but turned out to be anything but, these weekly gatherings are clearly focused. During the meetings there are prayers for the music and message that will be presented during the following four evenings of revival. Then people fan out across the church's large sanctuary, walking down each aisle and touching each pew, praying for the people who will be coming to Brownsville to meet God, and "sweeping" evil and demonic forces from the room.

In addition, church member Jeanie Bush coordinates an all-volunteer prayer team that meets in the church's choir room half an hour before every revival service to ask God's blessing on each night's meeting. Evangelist Steve Hill often participates in these pre-revival prayer meetings, and he says it is prayer that causes people to respond to his messages, not any outstanding oratorical ability.

"I'm a mediocre preacher at best," says Hill. "But it's because these people have been praying for me, and for all of the people who attend these revival services, that anything happens here."

Seeing with a Pastor's Eyes

When revival finally hit on Father's Day 1995, Kilpatrick was swept up in the spiritual frenzy as much as anyone, falling onto his back near the pulpit and staying down for nearly four hours. But during most of the hundreds of revival services since that day, the six-foot-two man carefully scans the sanctuary, looking for anything that seems worldly, wicked, or just plain weird.

During a typical night of revival, thousands of people can be singing their hearts out to God. Some dance in the aisles, while others stand quietly by the church's cushioned pews, singing with arms raised to heaven and tears streaming down their faces. Still others are deep in prayer, their eyes closed and their heads looking down. But not Kilpatrick. No matter how rowdy things in the sanctuary get, he typically stands still and silent, his eyes exploring every millimeter of the crowded room like a hawk looking for a rodent.

"I'm scanning the church and looking with the eyes of a pastor," he says. "If I see something that's disruptive, something that's fleshly, or something that's a distraction, my ushers just look at me and they know what to do."

Those who are emotionally acting out, flailing around with no respect to anyone around them, or drawing attention to themselves through unusual manifestations may find themselves in the firm but gentle grasp of one of Brownsville's watchful ushers, who escort unruly worshipers out into the hall, where they can carry on without disrupting the other two thousand souls seeking God in the sanctuary.

Usually there is no theological or spiritual judgment made when somebody is removed from the sanctuary. Kilpatrick and his ushers are not making a determination about how God is or is not working. It is simply a practical procedure inspired by a determination to follow St. Paul's simple dictum: "Let all things be done decently and in order" (1 Cor. 14:40).

"Pastor keeps the house clean," says Lindell Cooley.

However, Kilpatrick will come down on a church member who seems to prefer exotic manifestations over simple godly living. "There have been people before who sailed around the floor, but their lives were not in order," he says. "I would meet them by the pulpit and tell them, 'Go sit down. Your life just isn't right.'"

Kilpatrick is personally disgusted by outlandish manifestations, and he often says that between 10 and 25 percent of the acting out people do in his sanctuary is a result of emotional problems, fleshly experiences, or fakery. He does not always like everything he sees, but he is cautious about stepping in and stopping something unless he is sure it's not right. He does not want to play God and interfere with something that might be a true worship experience. "That's the thing I've fought for all these years," he says. "And when revival began, I had to swallow my pride and let God be God."

As Kilpatrick and others at Brownsville see it, God does not necessarily cause someone to fall to the floor. Instead, they view falling and other manifestations as people's responses to a touch from God. They are "outward, visible signs of an inner working of the Holy Spirit," he says. In addition to "falling under the power," Kilpatrick describes eight other categories of genuine manifestations in his book *When the Heavens Are Brass*:

- Shaking, jerking, or trembling, which can often be signs that God is cleansing a person of sin or sinful habits.
- Groaning and travailing, which may show that God is moving believers to pray more deeply.
- Deep bowing, which can be a sign of reverence or intercessory prayer.

- Heavy weeping and crying, which are responses to grieving and repentance for sin.
- Laughing, which though much less frequent at Brownsville than it is at Toronto, may be evidence of God granting a person forgiveness and freedom from inner pain or guilt.
- Being still or solemn, which may provide a level of intimate communion with God that one cannot achieve through rowdier responses.
- Being "drunk" in the Spirit, which—according to Kilpatrick—regardless of whether it happens to contemporary believers or the first Christians at pentecost, "occurs after spending a lengthy time in the Lord's presence. You sense the Holy Spirit so strongly that normal activity is difficult to perform."
- Having visions and dreams, which may come while a worshiper is "resting in the Lord."

Only God knows the complex causes of each of these varied manifestations. And typically, Brownsville leaders try to strike a balance between cutting people some slack and not allowing one person's disruptive behavior to bother everybody else. As Kilpatrick told me:

Suppose a girl of nineteen comes in here who has never been loved in her life. She's never had her mama brush her hair. She's never had her daddy tie the sash on the back of her dress. When she comes in here and gets touched by the love of God, she's going to have a powerful response to that.

Now if I stand there like some harsh monitor and say, "Hey! Stop that!" I've destroyed that girl. But if I'm patient, and watch her over the next few nights, she'll probably calm down.

Perhaps surprisingly, Kilpatrick is extremely tolerant when a person believed to be demon-possessed writhes and makes a commotion in his church. Such episodes happen on occasion at Brownsville, particularly when Hill preaches about deliverance. And even though Kilpatrick cringes inside, and worries about what visiting pastors might think, he does not do anything that might interfere with a person's chance to be freed from demonic oppression or possession.

> When that happens, my pride as a pastor goes, *Oh, God!* But where else do these people need to be? They need to be delivered. And I believe a church should be a spiritual hospital, not a museum.
>
> You don't condone everything that happens, but you can't be quick to condemn everything, either. I'm evaluating constantly.

Drawing once again on his rich trove of biblical and agrarian imagery, Kilpatrick teaches that the pastor is a shepherd of God's sheep. While sheep walk on all fours, he says, a godly pastor stands upright and tries to see things the sheep can't see. And he believes the pastor's two main tools are the shepherd's rod and staff. The staff, with its big crook, is used to guide and direct the sheep. The rod is used to scare away or beat off those who would attack the flock.

Over the years Kilpatrick has often used the shepherd's rod. He does not let people involved in adultery or homosexual relationships sing in the choir or serve in the church. And a year before revival broke out, he shut down a visiting evangelist who had a "strange" spirit and who stirred up the congregation with fake revival-type manifestations.

In 1992 Kilpatrick had asked Michael Griffin, a member of the church, to find another church home. Griffin made history in March 1993 by shooting Dr. David Gunn outside a Pensacola abortion clinic. Gunn became the first U.S. doctor to be killed during an anti-abortion demonstration, and Griffin is currently serving a life sentence for the crime.

Long before this violent episode occurred, Kilpatrick knew Griffin was trouble waiting to happen. "He had extremely narrow-minded views about some things," says Kilpatrick, who hesitates to be more specific about what those views were, only to say that they were not about abortion. "I told him that unless he turned from his extremist views, he had better find another church. I turned him out."

Griffin's wife and two daughters still attend Brownsville, but those who know the family say they and other Brownsville members do not share Griffin's radical views.

In July 1994 Dr. John Britton and a bodyguard were killed outside a Pensacola abortion clinic by Paul Hill, a Christian who had no connection to Brownsville. Some pro-abortion groups claim that Brownsville is a hotbed of anti-abortion activism. And while Kilpatrick and Hill often preach about abortion as a grave personal and social sin, they strongly deny the charge that they induce or support clinic violence.

Harsh Words

Those who understand how Kilpatrick feels about protecting and guarding his church were not completely surprised when he reacted the way he did after critic Hank Hanegraaff attacked the Brownsville revival on nationwide TV.

Hanegraaff, president of the Christian Research Institute, had been invited to appear on CNN's *Larry King Live* on Friday, April 4, 1997, to discuss the recent suicides of thirty-nine members of the Heaven's Gate cult, a San Diego–area group that subscribed to a bizarre mix of UFO theories and pseudo-Christian heresies. The members' bodies were found on March 26, along with notes and videos saying they were shedding their human "containers" for a trip to a "level beyond human" in a spaceship hidden from view behind the Hale-Bopp comet.

Hanegraaff told King's nationwide audience that spiritual

deception was not the sole property of non-Christian cults like Heaven's Gate, but could be found in mainstream Christian churches like Brownsville, which he said practiced "psychosocial manipulation" and "altered states of consciousness." According to Hanegraaff, Heaven's Gate and the Brownsville revival were really two sides of the same coin: the slide away from rational, revealed religion toward feeling-oriented fantasies.

Two days later, Kilpatrick lashed out at Hanegraaff during his Sunday sermon, criticizing him for acting like "the high sheriff of heaven" and warning him to stop criticizing the revival:

> Hank Hanegraaff, you may feel like you've put on the badge of heaven and put on your white cap and saddled up your big horse to ride through the kingdom of God to straighten everybody out. But I am going to tell you one thing. You may criticize other people and other moves of God and other ministries. But you had better leave your hands off this one.

In addition, Kilpatrick warned that unless Hanegraaff stopped criticizing the revival, his southern California–based Christian Research Institute would fall in ninety days.

Far from silencing Hanegraaff, Kilpatrick's words only egged him on. Hanegraaff repeatedly played Kilpatrick's comments on his "Bible Answer Man" radio show, which airs on hundreds of Christian stations. In addition, Hanegraaff instituted a daily countdown in which he satirically told listeners how many days the ministry had left before God shut it down.

Kilpatrick broke the ugly stalemate on June 18, issuing a three-page statement, admitting he was wrong for attacking his attacker, and asking Hanegraaff to forgive him.

> I do sincerely humble myself and ask your forgiveness for un-Christlike behavior. I repent before Jesus, and I've asked Him to

forgive me. I pray you will forgive me, and I also ask the body of Christ to forgive me. I was wrong.

Thus far Hanegraaff has not offered any public apologies for his harsh comments about Brownsville, but he has softened his criticism and established cordial relations with Kilpatrick and other Brownsville revival leaders.

Today Kilpatrick looks back at the whole episode with regret. "It was wrong, and I knew it was wrong," he says. "But his comments upset me. They got my indignation up. I reacted the way a mother dog does when someone fools with her puppies."

Kilpatrick has also responded to Hanegraaff's charge that the pastor's original comments had been issued as a prophecy. According to Hanegraaff, the fact that Kilpatrick's warnings about CRI did not come to pass means that Kilpatrick should be considered a "false prophet." But Kilpatrick says his words were not intended to be heard as prophecies. "I did not say, 'Thus saith the Lord.' It was, 'Thus saith John Kilpatrick.'"

Hanegraaff has continued to criticize the Brownsville revival, but he cooled down some of his more heated rhetoric following a December 1997 visit to Brownsville. Although he had visited the church before, this was the first time he and revival leaders put aside their high-profile posturing and engaged in frank, private talks. Although these talks did little to change anyone's views, they did help foster a new level of communication. And during the talks Kilpatrick even invited Hanegraaff to preach at one of Brownsville's Sunday services, an offer Hanegraaff told me he was considering.

How Revival Happens

Believers have been praying to God for revival for centuries. But in the early 1830s, Charles Finney gave a series of lectures that suggested that people could do more than pray: they could prepare and plan. Finney's "New Measures" changed the way people of his day looked at revival, and they have had a dramatic impact on the way believers have understood the subject ever since.

"A revival is not a miracle, nor dependent on a miracle, in any sense," said Finney in his talks, which were published in 1835 under the title *Revival Lectures*. "It is a purely philosophical result of the right use of constituted means." Finney spoke extensively about the proper "means" to use, spelling out which types of sermons, music, prayers, and altar calls that had proven to be most effective.

At times Finney made the whole process sound so methodical, so mechanical that it seemed God was not even part of it. But before dismissing him as a crass materialist, listen to his insistence that God must bless human efforts: "Means will not produce a revival, we all know, without the blessing of God. No more will grain, when it is sown, produce a crop without the blessing of God."

Brownsville revival leaders agree with much of what Finney has to say, especially his emphasis on prayer, a subject that occupies five of the twenty-two chapters in his published lectures. But they beg to differ with Finney on many other important points, including his insistence that revival is not miraculous.

Michael Brown has studied, prayed, and written about revival for fifteen years, and he is Brownsville's resident expert on the theology and history of revival. Brown speaks for the majority in Brownsville, as well as millions of believers elsewhere, when he claims that true awakening is "a God thing."

"You can no more schedule a revival than you can schedule an earthquake," said Brown during one Saturday evening revival service. "You can no more hold a revival than you can hold a hurricane. Revival is not something man works up. It's something God sends down."

Think of revival as a boat. Finney, on the one hand, might

suggest getting a souped-up outboard engine and setting out across the waves, asking God to bless the effort. Brown would rather hoist the sails and wait for the wind of God's Spirit to blow. If the boat didn't move, he would not remain passive; instead he would resort to using some oars. "We have to do what we can until the wind comes," he says. "Pull out the oars and row, but don't call it revival."

These differences, though they may seem merely semantic or superficial, are deep. And they matter.

Finney would charge Brown and others with allowing souls to perish in hell while waiting for God to swoop down and initiate something the church should be doing on its own. Critics of Finney, meanwhile, say reliance on proven methods leads to an overindulgence in revivalistic shenanigans such as grisly hellfire-and-brimstone sermons, manipulative altar calls, hyped-up hymn singing, and long, drawn-out "prayers," which are really thinly veiled preaching punctuated with occasional "Dear God's" and "we beseech Thee's." Such methods may bring scores of people to the altar, but do they provoke true spiritual transformation, or merely guilt?

For his part, Kilpatrick believes God brings revival when His people engage in persistent prayer, have a firm foundation in scriptural wisdom, expect to hear from God, and yield to His Spirit. Conversely, the five things Kilpatrick believes can hinder revival are doubt, distractions, disappointment, discouragement, and defamation.

Outsiders who have closely observed the Brownsville revival, however, come away convinced that revival would not have broken out here were it not for the deeply committed congregation that calls the church home. Almost overnight, Brownsville was transformed from a cozy, comfortable congregation to a busy, bustling bedlam of spiritually hungry sinners, road-weary visitors, and cramped conditions. While some members left, most have hung in there, welcoming the world to their church with open arms and supernatural patience.

One wonders what might happen in other churches if all the religious rhetoric about loving the lost became a big, boisterous reality?

"Revival is costly," says Kilpatrick, a man who in many ways has paid the cost.

Changed Lives

"The Lord gives me strength"

At sixty-seven years young, Earl Wingfield is just one of hundreds of loyal Brownsville members who have labored long hours behind the scenes.

The Squeaky Wheel Gets the Earl

Earl Wingfield was not looking for revival when he started attending Brownsville Assembly of God in 1990. At sixty-seven years of age, Earl was looking for an easy retirement after decades of working as an electronics technician at the Jacksonville Naval Air Station.

But ever since revival hit in 1995, Earl has been on the scene, putting in thirty to forty hours a week as one of the dozens of ushers struggling to keep up a modicum of church decorum in the midst of an invasion of millions. "We do maintain order," he says. Or as Brownsville member Steven Meek wrote in his poem, "Brother Earl,"

At the first little problem,
He's there on the spot,
To solve many problems,
To loosen many knots.

Earl puts in eight to twelve hours a day at the church Wednesdays through Fridays, leaving his home in Alabama after 3 P.M. and sometimes not getting back home until after 1 A.M. He puts in another five hours on Saturday mornings. "I get tired, but the Lord gives me strength," he says. "It's just something you do."

If you need a seat
And there's not one there,
He will go searching
To find you a chair.

When revival first hit, complete with people shaking and falling, Earl was a skeptic. But then, he says, God gave him the treatment specially reserved for skeptics. "I fell down beside my pew back by the sound booth," he says. "God did that to show me He can do whatever He wants to do. I am not critical any more. Let God do what He wants to do, and He knows what is real or fake." Earl says God gave him a "wonderful refreshing" while he was down. Another time, God healed him of acute muscle spasms in his back.

During most revival services the ever-vigilant Earl is so busy he does not catch much of what's going on around him.

He's the first one to answer
On the radio;
As you look about the room,
He's always on the go.

So Earl buys videotapes of the services and watches them at home. Like many longtime Brownsville members, it's the testimonies at the Friday evening baptismal services that touch him most deeply. "I weep just watching those testimonies," he says. "Here, we can see that lives are changed overnight."

One of the ushers' duties is to keep an eye on rowdy worshipers. "We're always observing, and we keep an eye on people who over-manifest. We sometimes remove them if they're hollering, or if they disturb other people."

He'll listen for the sound
Of off-beat tambourines;
You can count on him,
He is on the scene.

During the last three and a half years, Earl and most of the other Brownsville workers have had periods when they were tired and weary. But they keep on keeping on.

"It's a servant's job," he says. "You don't even think of what your rewards are. It just gives you a wonderful feeling of satisfaction to be a part of this revival. I believe this is one of the last great revivals that is going to hit this country before the Lord returns."

Earl has no idea when the revival will cool down, if ever. "This has already gone far beyond anything I ever expected," he says. "I think all of us have changed our thinking about who should come to church and who shouldn't. I just hope our facilities hold up."

Then suddenly, like a flash, Earl is gone. The interview is over. Perhaps somebody needs a chair.

So if you have a problem,
Give Brother Wingfield a whirl,
Because it is the squeaky wheel
That always gets the Earl.

Steve Hill was preaching when revival first broke out, and he's been delivering in-your-face, no-holds-barred sermons ever since.

CHAPTER FIVE

"Friend, Listen to Me!":

Evangelist Steve Hill

I t was evangelist Steve Hill who was preaching when revival broke out on Father's Day 1995 at Brownsville Assembly of God. And Steve Hill has been preaching at the evening revival services ever since.

Over the past three and one-half years, Hill has delivered more than seven hundred sermons. During that time he has probably paced at least seven hundred miles, striding furiously around the church's pulpit and marching up and down its broad carpeted aisles, stabbing the air with his finger, mopping sweat off his face with a handkerchief, and confronting his listeners with both the good news and the bad news of the gospel: the mercies of God for those who accept Christ, and fires of hell for those who don't.

"Friend, listen to me!" he often says when beginning a sermon or moving to a new point. And this simple comment captures the essence of a Steve Hill sermon.

Hill views everyone as his friend, and possibly even God's friend. His approach is warm and accepting, and he explicitly welcomes addicts, prostitutes, and even witches to hear his words. But his message is also urgent and passionate. "Listen to me," he says, conveying that those who don't are taking a great and eternal risk.

Ask people who listen to Hill what they *enjoy* about his

preaching and you will hear high praise for a variety of things: his sense of humor, his clear communication style, his colorful stories, and his frequent allusions to his own sordid past. "If God could save him, He can save anybody," they say, repeating nearly word-for-word a message Hill frequently delivers himself.

But ask them what it is they believe makes his preaching so *effective*, and there's much greater unanimity. "It's his passion for souls," they say. "You can feel it."

Steve Hill is a man who—whether preaching before the crowds at Brownsville or chatting casually with you in his office—can begin weeping without warning. He says the tears spring from a deep sorrow for lost souls, both those suffering eternal torment in hell and those living through hell in the here-and-now. When Hill begins to weep, his piercing blue eyes go all soft and sensitive, and tears begin to cascade down his face.

"I'm tired of people going through so much unnecessary struggle," he explains between sobs, dabbing his reddened face with that ever-present handkerchief. "I'm sick of seeing people become alcoholics and drug addicts. I'm sick of needless deaths on the highways. I'm sick of little girls being sexually abused by their fathers. I'm sick of teenagers being sucked into prostitution because of drug addiction."

The tears slow to a trickle as Hill thinks back to the pains he both endured and caused others as a drug addict, petty thief, and all-around "nasty person." "I went through a lot myself," he recalls, "and a lot of it was brought on by myself.

"But when I found how wonderful it was to be free, I determined to spend the rest of my life letting others know they don't have to live in bondage."

It was nearly a quarter-century ago that Hill, suffering in his own private hell, called on the name of Jesus and began "going for God." Since then he has handed out evangelistic tracts on street corners, traveled around the globe to speak at rallies and crusades, and preached to the more than two million people who have attended the Brownsville revival. For one and all, his message has been simple and timeless: *I once was lost, but now am found, and you, too, can find what I found.* Hill's sermons are delivered with the unshakable faith of one who has been snatched from the flames by God's loving hand.

"Friend," he says in one sermon, "all the words and arguments in the world won't move me one inch because I've personally experienced a miraculous deliverance and salvation through Jesus Christ. My life is living proof—evidence of a God who saves lost souls."

Since 1995 Hill has become a religious superstar, but he says he cares less about being in newspapers than he does being honored in heaven and feared in hell.

"All I want to do is be a sickle in God's hands," he says. "I would be honored to carry that role."

Calling on the Name of Jesus

There was shock and even some degree of skepticism when twenty-one-year-old Steve Hill wrote his older sister Marcia and told her God had delivered him from crime and addiction. It was 1975, and Steve had spent most of the previous five years in a substance-induced haze.

"My brother was a drug addict growing up," says Marcia Pate, who runs a child-care center and lives with her husband, Dan, in Huntsville, Alabama. "All I had heard since I had left home was that Mama was having a hard time with Steve. And things only got worse after our father died in 1970. My approach was to watch him and see how he did."

Her skepticism was understandable. Since he was thirteen, Steve had been smoking dope, popping pills, and injecting narcotics he and others had stolen from local pharmacies—hobbies that landed him in jail numerous times. Marcia says Steve's sense of humor, his friendly nature, and his innate leadership abilities meant that many local kids followed Steve in his misdeeds.

As he writes in his testimony book, *Stone Cold Heart*, Steve believed he would wind up dead, as some of his friends did, but there was nothing he could do to slow his descent. "The cycle of drugs-crime-jail, drugs-crime-jail repeated over and over—only to be stopped by death itself."

In 1997 the *Pensacola News Journal* reported that Hill had fabricated much of his testimony and overstated his life of drugs and crime, a charge he vehemently denies. Those who knew Hill during his troubled years say his published testimony barely scratches the surface.

"We were all aware of his problems," says Joy Rodgers, a registered nurse and longtime family friend from Huntsville who once helped resuscitate a druggy Hill. After seeing the *News Journal* article, Rodgers wrote the following account:

> One fall afternoon in 1975 Steve's mother called me to see if I could help him. Steve was propped up in his bed, surrounded by boxes of morphine tubexes. He had four half-empty syringes still stuck in his veins. There was an empty sleeping pill bottle on the bed next to him. His pupils were pin points. His skin was gray and cold to the touch. His nail beds were blue. His respirations were approximately two per minute . . . Thank God he was able to overcome his problems and come back from the brink of death.

Hill's spiritual rebirth happened on October 28 of the same year, when his mom asked for help from her Lutheran minister, who visited Steve and told him, "I can't help you, but I know somebody who can. His name is Jesus, and He's here with us."

Hill began calling out to Jesus, and soon those now-famous tears began to fall. "Tears that had been bottled up during fifteen years of rebellion, hurt, and bitterness suddenly began to flow like a river down my cheeks," he says. "A peace—a warmth such as I never felt before—filled my body."

If Hill's life story were to be made into a corny evangelistic movie, the cameras would cut from this dramatic conversion to a panoramic shot of a triumphant Hill preaching before the masses. But instead of going directly from the darkness of his room to the bright lights of Brownsville, Hill went back to jail once again, the result of outstanding narcotics warrants. During the months he spent behind bars, Hill's gloom and confusion were lifted during regular visits from evangelist Jim Summers of Outreach Ministries of Alabama.

Summers, who began reaching out to troubled young people in the 1960s, said people had warned him about Hill. "They told me to leave him alone," he says. "They said he was just scum." Summers recalls that Hill did look pretty bad the first time he saw the youngster. He vividly recalls Hill as half-hippie, half-redneck, sporting a muscle T-shirt, bell-bottom pants, long frizzy hair, and big bare feet. But Summers hung in there with Hill. And when he visited a recently converted Hill in jail, he was moved by the change in his life. "I saw something in Steve I had never seen in anybody else," he recalls. "He was intense about serving the Lord."

Hill was released from jail and probated to Outreach Ministries, where for the next three months Summers gave him a steady diet of spiritual discipleship and harsh discipline. Next, Hill spent nine months in Cape Girardeau, Missouri, at a program run by Teen Challenge, an international ministry founded by Assemblies of God minister David Wilkerson. Then Hill attended Twin Oaks Academy, a Texas-based Teen Challenge leadership training school, where he learned more about evangelizing the lost. At Twin Oaks, Hill also met his future wife, Jeri, who has her own torrid testimony and zeal for serving God.

After their marriage, the couple moved to Panama City, and then Tallahassee, Florida, where Hill served as a church youth minister. But soon Hill was sensing that God might be calling him to minister elsewhere. Meanwhile, once-skeptical sister Marcia was finally beginning to believe.

"Steve phoned me and said something was calling him and Jeri, and the next thing I knew they had sold everything they owned and left the country," she recalls. "I don't think he could pull off things like this if he wasn't directed by God. Now I can say that every single thing I've seen my brother say and do since he gave his life to Christ has been sincere."

It was while he was a youth pastor that Hill took his kids on a short-term missions trip to Mexico. The trip was designed to expose the young people to life and ministry on foreign soil, but the trip wound up changing Hill's life perhaps more than it influenced his kids.

> I remember standing on a Mexico City street corner with a box of tracts. People would line up to get a tract, and then they would stand up against a nearby wall and read them. I stood there and cried. Then I prayed, "God, I'm from a country where when you hand someone a tract, nine-tenths of them throw it into a waste basket. But here there's such hunger. Jesus, speak to me."

Jesus spoke, and Hill listened, pulling up his Florida roots and leaving for seven years of evangelism and church planting in Argentina for the Assemblies of God's foreign missions division. From 1985 to 1992 he worked with famed Argentinean evangelist Carlos Anacondia, whose crusades have reportedly led a million souls to Christ.

In 1992 the Hills returned to America, founding their Together in the Harvest ministry and moving to Lindale, Texas, where Steve could receive guidance from mentor Leonard Ravenhill. From 1992 to 1995 Hill traveled to Spain, Columbia, Belarus, and other countries to preach, teach, and set up churches. He also preached at American churches like Brownsville.

Brownsville would have been just another stop on Hill's preaching itinerary. The only difference was that the Brownsville revival didn't stop, and Hill didn't leave. Instead, he began canceling all his other engagements. In 1996, when it seemed the revival might continue even longer, he relocated his family and ministry to a forty-acre farm in Lillian, Alabama. The complex has a house where Hill and his family live and other nearby houses, which provide office and residential space for the ministry's eleven full-time and three part-time employees.

For Hill's older brother George, who had once been as shocked and skeptical about his brother's conversion as sister Marcia had, Steve's role in the Brownsville revival seems like a natural progression from his international evangelism work. "It's an amazing transformation he's had," says George, who lives in California, gave his life to the Lord in 1995, and was baptized at Brownsville in 1997.

"He's been down the wrong road and he knows what that's like. He's been there and he's believable. He's been walking with the Lord so long that this revival is a natural for him."

Standing on Others' Shoulders

Steve Hill's office is not one of those sterile, industrial-looking rooms that one might see parodied in a Dilbert cartoon. Instead, Hill's sanctum, which takes up the master bedroom of one of the single-story houses at Together in the Harvest's Lillian complex, is a repository of material about revivalism and a monument to past moves of God.

In one corner stands a heavy, wooden pulpit that was used in the 1800s and picked up by Hill at a flea market. The wood is dark. The platform where a Presbyterian preacher set his Bible and his notes is smoothed from decades of use. And the right-and left-hand ledges, which the pastor gripped during thousands of sermons, are worn down from regular use.

Surrounding the pulpit are towering bookshelves containing some three thousand books, half of them published before 1900. Hill giddily removes a huge, heavy 1684 edition of *Foxe's Book of Martyrs* from an oversized shelf. "This hasn't been abridged like the modern editions," he says.

The theme of dying for Christ is picked up in one of the framed paintings and prints that hang in the study. *The Martyrs*, a vivid drawing that shows Christians being mauled by lions in a Roman amphitheater, hangs prominently on one wall. The room is also decorated with hats worn by Salvation Army workers during the last century, and other evangelistic antiques and knickknacks.

"I love the 1800s," says Hill. "And I like to surround myself with church history. I can feel the presence of the Lord here."

Hill draws inspiration from leaders of historic revivals of the past and studies the sermons of preachers like George Whitefield and Jonathan Edwards.

When preparing his own messages, Hill asks God for guidance and engages in a process of ruthless self-examination. Here's how he described the process in one of his books.

In order to preach correctly, I always take three looks before every sermon:

1. at my own sinfulness;
2. at the depth of human wretchedness all around me; and
3. at the love of God in Christ Jesus.

After taking these three looks, I am:

1. empty of self; and
2. full of compassion toward those around me.

When Hill approaches the pulpit at Brownsville, there is one final step he takes before his sermon. He did it that Father's Day, and he has done it some seven hundred times since. He leads the congregation in the recitation of this simple prayer: "Dear Jesus, speak to my heart, change my life, in Your precious name, Amen."

Preaching to "Whosoever" Will Hear

Steve Hill still has a few sermons to go before he reaches the numbers of George Whitefield, the voice of America's first Great Awakening, who preached some eighteen thousand times and reached an estimated ten million hearers.

But Hill is fascinated by Whitefield and imitates his simple and direct preaching style. Unlike Whitefield, however, Hill does prepare copious notes for each of his sermons—sometimes twenty pages' worth or more. Still, he's more than happy to dispense with his outline when he feels God leading him to do so, as he did during one 1998 revival service. "The Lord spoke to me about this sermon. He said, 'Do not cloud the issue. Do not cause My people to be overwhelmed with much when what I have to say is simple.'"

Simplicity is a watchword for Hill, whose uncomplicated title for a sermon based on James 4:1–7 was "God Snubs Snots."

This may be ridiculously simple for some of you, but it's profound . . . You don't need a Greek lexicon or a degree in biblical languages to understand what it means. In fact, it is so simple that we usually miss it: God resisteth the *proud*, but He giveth grace to the *humble*.

Nor is Hill opposed to theatrics. "White Cane Religion" is probably Hill's most popular sermon, selling thousands of copies in audiotape, video, and printed versions. Based on Matthew 15:14 ("if the blind leads the blind, both will fall into a ditch"), the sermon features Hill with a blind man's dark glasses and white cane stumbling around the Brownsville pulpit.

He also used elaborate props for his moving 1998 sermon, "No Time to Wash Up," which was based on Revelation 19:9 ("Blessed are those who are called to the marriage supper of the Lamb!"). To demonstrate the need for spiritual purity, Hill daubed a wedding dress with mud. He then asked that the sanctuary lights be dimmed and spotlights turned on his wife, Jeri, who walked down the aisle toward the pulpit in a clean wedding dress as the sounds of a popular wedding march blared from the church's sound system. Hundreds of people rushed to the altar to seek forgiveness and cleansing at the sermon's end.

Some have derided Hill's back-to-basics approach. One critic even suggested that the evangelist uses Scripture more as a jumping-off point for a series of personal anecdotes rather than the foundation of his message. But Hill is more worried about confronting sinners and the backslidden with the reality of a righ-teous God than he is about pleasing Christian critics. And at times he seems to bend over backward to let everyone know that the gospel is relevant.

"There's hope for everyone in this room," he said during one 1996 sermon, and then he launched into a five-hundred-word recitation he calls his "whosoever" passage. Published in *The God Mockers*, a collection of Hill's sermons, the passage is a classic piece of Hill prose designed to show that God sent His Son to die for everyone, including:

You'ns, y'all, us'ns, we, we'ns, you's guys, you guys, all, each person, that individual, all the people, kids, adolescents, old folks, young folks, city slickers, farm boys, home boys, hamburger flippers, ice cream dippers, teeter totter riders, fearless skydivers, short order cooks and collectors of books, smart people that teach, and mooches that leach, Michiganders from Kalamazoo, and citizens of Timbuktu, butchers and bakers, and candlestick makers, anybody can be saved. "Whosoever," that is you!

You can be big, tall, small, short, full-headed, gray-headed, bald headed, headed for bald headed, big boned, medium boned, small boned, blond hair, black hair, red hair, green hair, gross hair, red, yellow, black, or white. You are precious in His sight.

You can be sort of bad, sort of real bad, really bad, baddest of bad, or king of bad.

You can live uptown, downtown, out of town, suburbs, big house, small house, no house, jailhouse, little house on the prairie, penthouse in Pittsburgh, Days Inn in downtown Dayton . . .

You can be a Jew from Jerusalem or a Gentile from Jacksonville. You can play the banjo or be named Joe and play in a band. You can be so smart that you can say the ABCs backward or be so backward that you never learned the ABCs. You can hold the Guinness Book of World Records for eating the most live slugs or have a collection of the world's most colorful bugs. You can be visiting this revival like everyone "oughta" or come walking off the streets from Boston just to get a drink of "wata."

You can be patriotic, wearing red, white, and blue and be sitting by your friend who has a big tattoo. You can be a shepherd from the hills or a pusher of pills, a wise man from afar or a soap opera star. You can be a Methodist from Montana or a Jew from Japan, be a vegetarian from Virginia or a connoisseur of Spam. You can come from Texas in a Lexus with spurs in your heels, or be a fly fisherman from Frankfurt with 15 shiny reels.

You can make your living churning delicious homemade butter, or spend every day collecting cans in the gutter. You can play a guitar and be an international star, or be a clown in a circus driving the world's smallest car. You can be the tidiest person this world has ever known, or live like a pig with garbage in your home.

You can keep up with the Joneses or be the Jones's housekeeper or maybe the coolest dude in school with the largest florescent beeper. You can smell like Chanel and live like a queen, or make your abode in an alley wearing tattered Levi's jeans. You can drive a BMW and wear flashy Italian suits or ride an Appaloosa sporting pointed cowboy boots.

It doesn't make a difference if you're happy or you're blue, just call upon the Lord—"whosoever," that's you!

If there are people within the range of Hill's voice who miss the point that Jesus died for them, it is not for his lack of trying.

Rescuing Souls from the Fires of Hell

In his office Hill has a big, leather-bound collection of Jonathan Edwards's sermons that was published in 1879. The New England minister preached more than one thousand sermons, and most of them were about God's love and mercy. But Edwards is best known for his now-classic sermon, "Sinners in the Hands of an Angry God," which he preached to great effect in Enfield, Connecticut, on July 8, 1741. Here is an excerpt:

> The God that holds you over the pit of hell, much as one holds a spider, or some loathsome insect, over the fire, abhors you, and is dreadfully provoked: his wrath towards you burns like fire; he looks upon you as worth of nothing else, but to be cast into the fire . . . you are ten thousand times more abominable in his eyes, than the most hateful venomous serpent is on ours . . . and yet, it is nothing but his hand that holds you from falling into the fire every moment . . .
>
> And now you have an extraordinary opportunity, a day wherein Christ has thrown the door of mercy wide open, and stands calling, and crying with a loud voice to poor sinners.

Steve Hill has studied Edwards's sermons, and he frequently confronts his listeners with vivid pictures of the reality of hell. One of his sermons is called "Our Loving Savior Will Also Be a Severe Judge." And another, "Pulled from the Fire," gives sinners an opportunity to mend their ways:

> The fire alarm has sounded: there's fire in the house. It is time to escape the flames of sin. Don't complain about the irritating volume of God's alarm—it is the sound of your salvation . . . I suppose God could have used a "softer, gentler" alarm, but He chose me and told me to preach loudly and urgently. I don't preach a "toned down" or politically correct gospel; I just shout at the top of my lungs, "There's fire in the house! Get out while you can!"

Or as he says in his sermon, "The God Mockers": "I am intense and the situation is urgent, because this is a matter of life and death."

As journalist Mark Schone wrote in "An Awesome God," his insightful article about the revival published in alternative rock music magazine *Spin*, "If Brownsville brings America back to God it will come on its knees, scared sinless. Steve Hill's message is harsh."

Hill is unapologetic. "Sometimes I feel like a surgeon," he says, "because I know that sometimes you have to make your patients hurt before they get better." And often Hill makes people feel bad about both the sin in their own lives and the moral decline they see all around them.

Effective evangelists have regularly tapped into the powerful but often unexpressed fears and anxieties that trouble their listeners. In 1665 a plague swept through London, killing thousands of people. Perhaps not surprisingly, a religious awakening followed soon after. On September 18, 1665, London minister Abraham Janeway preached these words during one of that year's many funeral sermons:

> Many thousands are fallen, and more thousands are like to fall; and who of you all, that are in your sins, can reasonably hope to

escape? . . . What peace can you find, when you have not made your peace with God, and you are in such danger every hour of being sent for to his judgment seat, by this grim messenger, whom none can resist? . . . Sinners, this night you may be in hell! Hell receiveth many guests tonight . . . Think what a thin veil of flesh is between you and eternity, how small and weak the thread of life is.

Half a century later and a continent away, Jonathan Edwards saw a warning from God in the rumblings of the earthquake of 1727. "Earthquakes and lights in the heaven may often have natural causes yet they may nevertheless be ordered to be as a forerunner of great changes and Judgments," he said in a sermon, adding that "our land is very defiled" by an "abundance of cheating and injustice."

For many of Hill's listeners it is not fear of the plague or worries about earthquakes that cause them anxiety. Rather, many are troubled by fears that America is losing its very soul and drifting into runaway secularism and rampant sin. Hill feels this anxiety himself, and it inspires some of his fieriest sermons. After witnessing a 1993 gay rights march in the nation's capital, Hill wrote in his journal:

My eyes have beheld the patient mercies of the Lord. If I had been in control of yesterday's march, if I had my hand on the handle opening the caverns of the earth, swallowing up the perversion, the lust, this abomination, there would have been no hope . . . How far can this country slip into the clutches of the enemy? It's racing toward judgment. Lord, you will have to apologize to Sodom and Gomorrah if this continues. It's an abomination. Yes, I have once again beheld the patience and mercies of God.

No Political Activist

Hill has political views, but he is not a political animal. After watching this gay rights march, he wept about the mysterious mercies of God; he did not go out and organize a local initiative drive. He did speak at an April 1997 Save the Commandments rally organized by conservative Alabama Governor Fob James, who was fighting to prevent the removal of the Ten Commandments from the wall of the building housing the state's Supreme Court. But Hill did not rally behind James's campaign; instead he presented the assembled politicians and other hearers with an invitation to accept Christ.

And Hill frequently talks about the sin of abortion, but he does not organize or participate in clinic protests or other pro-life crusades. If he were an activist, his sermons during January 1998 would have made note of the twenty-fifth anniversary of the U.S. Supreme Court's *Roe v. Wade* decision—a major milestone for the pro-life movement. But the anniversary went unnoticed in revival services.

The same month, shocking allegations surfaced that President Clinton had been sexually involved with a twenty-four-year-old White House intern. The national news media gave the scandal saturation coverage while Washington pundits debated the future of the presidency. But Hill avoided the temptation to engage in the popular religious-right pastime of Clinton bashing, but rather preached a message of repentance. The evangelist looked straight into the camera located in the center of the sanctuary balcony, and said, "Whether these allegations are true or not, Bill Clinton, God can forgive you."

Like most contemporary pentecostals, Hill is at about the same place today that most evangelicals were three decades ago: resolutely apolitical and zealously committed to changing the world by saving individual souls.

He is far less concerned about the sexual shenanigans of people wielding power in Washington than he is about the spiritual unfaithfulness of people sitting in the pews. "We've committed spiritual adultery," says Hill. "Some of you have entertained things you shouldn't have. Well, you've entertained too far."

And not even religiosity is enough to save someone from the wrath of God. "Religion will damn your soul," he screams. Then he repeats one of the revival's most famous Hill-isms: "Religion is hanging around the cross, but true Christianity is getting on the cross." The slogan has been emblazoned on T-shirts, which are sold by a man working from a trailer outside the bingo hall across from the church. But Hill is not through raging against religiosity yet.

> You can go to hell with baptismal waters on your face and a confirmation certificate hanging on the wall behind your desk. You can go to hell even though you were the most faithful Sunday school teacher in your denomination and a founding member of the largest church in the city! Answer this question: *Do you know Jesus?*

And if Protestant pieties cannot save you, turning to other faiths is not any better. "Mohammed and Buddha didn't die for you. And for those of you who call 1-900-PSYCHIC, they don't care about you. If they cared about you, it would be 1-800-PSYCHIC."

Preaching as if It Mattered

Neither Steve Hill's preaching nor the rest of the whole Brownsville revival experience is for everyone. Both are heavily colored by their roots in southern pentecostalism, and Hill would be the first to admit that these influences may contribute to a unique, if not peculiar, religious dialect that may limit their appeal, no matter how much they wish to communicate Christ to any and all.

Still, there is much about Hill's preaching that can be instructive for anyone seeking better ways to communicate to "whosoever." Here are four practical ideas to consider.

Preach with Passion

Hill either cares very much about his message and the people he is passing it on to, or somebody should give the man an honorary Oscar! He paces, hollers, points, gesticulates, paces some more, pleads, thunders, and preaches himself nearly hoarse. While some may quibble with his style, there is no denying the passion he feels for the gospel and the compassion he feels for those he is addressing.

"Some of you may have a problem with a preacher who says he hears from Jesus," he said during one 1998 sermon. "But if you're a preacher and you don't hear from God, I have a problem with you."

Talk to the People

Unfortunately, some ministers seem to prepare and deliver their sermons as if they are still trying to get a positive evaluation from their divinity school deans. There are the requisite three points and the off-the-shelf illustrations; there are lofty-sounding references to the Hebrew and the Greek; and often there are pews full of people wondering about what they're going to have for lunch, or who will win today's game, or why they even go to church.

Call Hill's sermons plain and simple if you like, and criticize his rhetorical excesses while you're at it. But don't dismiss the fact that his sermons, which would be ridiculed at many seminaries, connect with people. Like "Crazy" Moody (which is how some of his contemporaries derisively referred to famed evangelist Dwight Moody), Hill's sermons are unapologetically homey and sentimental. As a result, they have an ability to help hardened sinners see the love of God, or help pew-sitting Pharisees get a sense of how God wants their devotion. Hill preaches (and members of Brownsville pray) as if the lives of some of the people out there listening may actually be transformed as a result, and that's not a bad approach.

Find a Partner

Steve Hill and John Kilpatrick make a wonderful team. Hill is the radical rabble-rouser, while Kilpatrick is the conservative pastor. And their affection for each other is deep and apparent. They say they are not envious of each other's work, and their frequent public pledges of love and support—which are a true joy to behold—seem to bear that out.

"Two are better than one," says the wise author of Ecclesiastes. Being a pastor or an evangelist can be a lonely life. What is worse, spiritual isolation can lead to secret sin or "sudden" falls. If you cannot find a strong ministry partner like Hill and Kilpatrick have found in each other, perhaps you can seek more diligently for a spiritual confidant or mentor with whom you can exchange joys and sorrows, triumphs and failings.

Lead Others to a Living God

There is a burgeoning spiritual hunger in America these days, with religious themes weaving themselves through much of contemporary popular culture and with booming sales for books about finding one's spiritual path—no matter how twisting and turning that path may be.

Unfortunately, most American churches have been unable to tap into that vast hunger, and that is due, at least in part, to the fact that most of them proclaim not a living God but a dead, dreary orthodoxy. "God is Spirit," wrote John, "and those who worship Him must worship in spirit and truth (4:24 NKJV)." That does not mean everyone has to adopt Brownsville's pentecostal approach. But it may mean more people might come forward to altars in other churches if they believed there would be a big, beautiful, living God to meet them there.

Changed Lives

Saved from the pits of hell

Robert Lowell's wealth barely concealed a life of addiction and despair. Now, deadness has been replaced by overwhelming joy.

Having It All Wasn't Enough

Robert and JoAnn Lowell had it all. Robert was president of Georgia Credit and Collections Bureau, Inc., a big and profitable collection agency. JoAnn was a senior director with Mary Kay Cosmetics. The Lowells and three of their five children lived in a large house in Blairsville, two hours north of Atlanta, and they were regulars at a Baptist church, where Robert sang in the choir and joined other men in praying before church on Sunday mornings.

But just beneath the surface, things were a mess. JoAnn was an insecure workaholic whose relationship with God had to accommodate her hectic schedule. Robert was addicted to cigarettes, alcohol, and prescription drugs. He also suffered from depression, insomnia, paranoia, and migraine headaches. At work and at home, he was a lying, manipulative tyrant who used rage, sarcasm, and verbal abuse to get his way.

JoAnn first attended revival services at Brownsville in the fall of 1995. "The praise and worship was electrifying," she recalls. "During the course of the evening I was prayed for a number of times, each time falling to the floor. I lay on the floor for hours and was there until the lights dimmed and it was time to leave."

In January 1996 JoAnn was to attend a Mary Kay meeting in San Antonio. But she went back to Brownsville instead. This time, her experience of the presence of God was even deeper. "God's love so flooded my heart and His presence was so near, everything else in comparison quickly faded." During an intense period of praise and worship, JoAnn ventured out into the aisle and began dancing to God, a first for her. "At some point during this time I was delivered from the bondage of the fear of man."

Meanwhile, Robert was confused and angry. He hopped into his car in Blairsville and drove through a raging snowstorm to Pensacola. "I didn't want to be at this church," he says. "I just wanted to get my wife and save her from this fanaticism."

Entering the sanctuary, Robert "felt as though everyone was looking at me. I was angry and mad at JoAnn for sitting up front. I watched the pastor and the evangelist and told JoAnn they were all about money. I was sure these men were after my wife. The more it went on, the angrier I got. When several men came over to greet me, including the pastor, I knew I was a marked man and my wife had set me up."

After Steve Hill's sermon, pastor John Kilpatrick invited married couples down front to receive prayer—the first time he had ever done so in revival services. Robert and JoAnn went forward. Kilpatrick prayed for the couple, put his arms around Robert, and told him Jesus loved him. "He hugged me and squeezed about fifteen to twenty-five years of nastiness out of me," recalls Robert. "I felt these thousand-pound weights go off me."

But Robert was still struggling inside. He made a break for the back door of the sanctuary only to encounter Hill there. "Steve Hill walked straight over to me, touched my shoulder, and knocked me about five feet up against the wall, where I landed in the corner. I slid down the wall and fell in a heap, where I stayed for a long time. God came over me and changed my life."

When he could stand up again, Robert found his wife and drove her to a nearby beach. There he asked Jesus to come into his heart and forgive his sins. "From that moment on, I was set free. God delivered me totally from my addictions. He took away the headaches and the insomnia. I sobbed for hours as we drove home together. God has taken out all the lying and anger and given me back honor and integrity. My marriage has been restored and all five children have forgiven me."

The Lowells decided to move to Pensacola so they could continue growing in the revival. JoAnn quit her job, and Robert changed his business practices to bring them in line with his newfound faith. Four of the couple's five children have visited the revival and reconciled with the Lord, and two are enrolled in classes at the Brownsville Revival School of Ministry.

When Robert was asked to give his testimony during a revival service, he could barely contain himself, expressing his joy in heartfelt language that had to be "bleeped" from the audio- and videotapes of the service—another revival first.

"I had all that I really wanted, but I really didn't have anything," he told the congregation between sobs and shouts of joy. "I think of all the years of my life I've wasted, being somebody I don't care to be any more. God has taken a man like me and saved me from the pits of hell. Yes! Now, I'm His vessel."

Worship leader Lindell Cooley often tunes out the din of the crowd to focus on his own worship of God.

CHAPTER SIX

Music to Wake the Dead:

Worship Leader Lindell Cooley

Long before the crowds at a Brownsville revival service hear evangelist Steve Hill preach, they are singing, dancing, clapping, jumping, laughing, and crying to the music of Lindell Cooley and the church's ten-member praise band.

And what music it is! Blending the raw power of old-timey pentecostal singin' and shoutin', the passion and soul of black gospel, and the latest contemporary Christian praise choruses, Cooley and company create a sound that resembles what might happen if a bus full of southern Assemblies of God musicians collided with Kirk Franklin and God's Property in the auditorium of a southern California megachurch.

A typical service might find the band and congregation joining together to sing pentecostal chestnuts like "My God Is Real," "The Happy Song" by youthful British praise band Delirious?, Richard Smallwood's rousing 1970s song "We've Come to Praise Him," and a few Vineyard choruses before closing with a chorus of "All Hail the Power of Jesus' Name" or another classic hymn.

"I just want to see everyone touched," says the slender, long-haired Cooley, who brings the same sense of personal mission to his music that Hill brings to his messages. "I know what God has done for me," Cooley says, "and I just want others to experience that for themselves."

Music prepares people to hear the sermon, and then after the message has been preached, more music helps drive home the sermon's message in a powerful, personal way. And that's the way it has been in the church for centuries.

But something slightly different happens when revival breaks out. Historically, the music created in the heat of spiritual awakening has spawned major new innovations in the way believers worship. Past revival song leaders like Ira Sankey and Homer Rodeheaver introduced memorable new melodies, creative ways of expressing timeless creeds in popular choruses, and bold and sometimes controversial arrangements and instrumentation. In the process, they changed the way Christians sang. More than a century ago, one observer noted:

> Every person conversant with revivals must have observed that whenever meetings for prayers and conference consume a special interest there is a desire for hymns and music of a different character from those ordinarily heard in church.

Cooley, a musician with deep roots in pentecostalism's musical and spiritual heritage, came to Brownsville two months before revival began. Now, three and a half years later, many say his moving music is the perfect complement to Hill's searing sermons. Cooley is not sure how much longer revival will last, but he is doing everything possible to create music that gives people plentiful opportunities to meet God themselves.

"There's such a spiritual hunger and awareness in the world today," he says. "I believe God will show up when we invite Him."

Singing in the Sheaves

If you have had the chance to attend one of Billy Graham's evangelistic crusades, or even if you've been able to see one of his numerous TV broadcasts, you'll know that one of the enduring images of these events is a stream of people rushing toward the altar as longtime Graham associate Cliff Barrows leads the crusade choir in the singing of "Just As I Am."

This classic gospel song is the perfect complement to Graham's evangelistic message. Its simple, heart-tugging message is married to an easy-to-sing but memorable melody in a way that stirs people's emotions and moves them to act on Graham's invitation. This one–two punch of message and music has been at the center of evangelistic efforts and revival movements for centuries.

Music has been at the heart of Christian worship and ministry since the first century, when Paul instructed believers to worship God with "psalms and hymns and spiritual songs, singing with grace in your hearts to the Lord" (Col. 3:16). The earliest Christians sang songs based on the Psalms or the faith's creeds, and these two sources provided the lyrics for a majority of the music believers offered to God for the next fifteen centuries.

In the 1500s the Protestant Reformation inspired a new style of singing and hymn writing, and some of the first Protestant hymnals were published. Still, many of these hymns were stilted and stodgy, at least until the time of Isaac Watts, who wrote more than four hundred hymns and Psalm paraphrases during the 1700s.

Watts, who gave religious music a new expressiveness, was criticized for the simplicity of his songs. But he defended his compositions, pointing out that they were designed to be sung by the masses, not to be debated by the elite: "I would neither indulge in any bold metaphors, nor admit of hard words, nor tempt the ignorant worshiper to sing without his understanding."

Many of Watts's simple and direct hymns were sung in America during America's Great Awakening. And some of his best-known numbers, such as "O God Our Help in Ages Past," which is based on Psalm 90, are still sung in Protestant and Catholic churches today, more than two and a half centuries after he wrote them.

If Watts provided much of the music for the Great Awakening, it was Charles Wesley who wrote the songs Americans were singing during the Second Great Awakening. The brother of evangelist John Wesley, Charles created some sixty-five hundred hymn texts, and composer George Frideric Handel, who is best known for his oratorio "The Messiah," provided the music for three. Wesley classics like "O For a Thousand Tongues to Sing" have long outlived the Second Great Awakening, and are still sung today around the world, and at the Brownsville revival.

Distinctive music is an important part of the heritage of the Salvation Army, the international group founded in London in 1865 by William and Catherine Booth, both of whom had been renewed by revival. The group's brass bands woke up the slums of London with their street-corner services, and can still be heard at some Salvation Army churches today.

Perhaps no single person has had a greater impact on the way revivals sound than Ira Sankey, the man whose skillful organ playing and expressive baritone voice were a regular feature of Dwight Moody's American and European crusades for more than two decades.

Sankey had a particular affinity for "story hymns," like "The Ninety and Nine," which combined basic Bible lessons with music adapted from popular dance songs and marches. Though Sankey wrote little himself, the collections of gospel songs he edited sold more than twenty million copies, changing church and revival services forever. (And Sankey did not succumb to the greed that would sink some later revivalists, pumping all the money he took in right back into Moody's ministry and school projects.)

Sankey and Moody created a model for cooperation between

evangelists and their song leaders, which would inspire many other musicians who ministered in the early twentieth century, including Charles Alexander, the music leader for evangelist R. A. Torrey, and Homer Rodeheaver, the composer and song leader for Billy Sunday. Like Sankey, Rodeheaver published songbooks for churches, an effort he hoped would liven up their often dull singing.

> Whenever I go around to churches I tell people there's no use in sitting around like a lot of sour crabapples scaring people away. We Christians have the right to be happy, so come on! Make this world a better and brighter place.

Lindell Cooley and the worshipers at the Brownsville revival are closest in style and theology to the Azusa Street revival of 1906–1909, which spawned the modern pentecostal movement. Although no single musician was a dominant figure of this revival, it did bring about new forms of music characterized by an unprecedented fervency and abandon.

In addition, pentecostals pioneered the use of tambourines, drums, and guitars—instruments that would be considered too wild for worship in most other Protestant churches until after the Jesus movement of the 1960s and 1970s ushered in a new wave of contemporary praise and worship music.

Today evangelists like Greg Laurie and Franklin Graham as well as organizers of the huge Promise Keepers rallies call on the services of the Maranatha! Praise Band, which is led by Jesus movement alumnus Tommy Coomes. And even Billy Graham's organization uses contemporary soloists in its crusades and aggressive bands like dc talk in its youth rallies.

Scenes from a Pentecostal Life

Lindell Cooley understands the important role music plays in the church, and his own life story is chock full of the kinds of supernatural miracles and unshakable, experiential faith that form the basis of much of pentecostal belief. "There are cases where God prepares people from the womb for specific tasks," he says, and he believes he is one such person, prepared to sing God's praises and help others to sing them too.

He considers his birth a divinely ordained event. His mother, Shirley, had lost two previous children—one in the third month of pregnancy, and a second that was born dead and nearly killed Shirley herself. She prayed, "Dear Heavenly Father, would You give me a child?" When Lindell was born, she declared him her "miracle child."

During the early months of Lindell's life, Shirley would rock him to sleep while praying over his hands. "Jesus, use these hands," she would pray. "Anoint these hands." Lindell believes such prayers gave him a unique blessing to make music for God. "I was introduced to the glory of the Lord at a very early age," he says.

When he was nine months old, the devil made the first of many attempts to destroy that blessing by trying to kill Lindell with a high fever. Following an all-night prayer marathon, Shirley says she saw angels hovering over Lindell's crib and heard the Lord tell her, "Don't fear. Your son is in My hands."

Lindell preached his first sermon at age five in a small, southern pentecostal church. And when he was ten, God saved him from another of the devil's attacks. Living in tiny Red Bay, Alabama, a town just down the road from nowhere, Lindell helped other local boys harvest their grandfather's watermelons. But tragedy struck when a trailer brimming over with a ton of melons ran over Lindell's body and head. Shirley brought Lindell home, prayed for him, and prescribed an unusual cure: "She put one Bible under my feet, another one under my back, and a third Bible under my head." Lindell awoke the next morning feeling fine and even more assured of God's hand on his life.

Throughout his youth, Lindell played music in churches

whenever he had the opportunity. And when his father, Gene, quit running from the call of God on his life and entered the ministry, Lindell had his first steady gig at his father's Red Bay church. Lindell played music there for the next seventeen years. During this period the church grew from 80 to 150 members.

Lindell also accompanied his mom when she sang at pentecostal revival meetings in tents across the South. Lindell still loves his parents deeply, dedicating his autobiographical book, *A Touch of Glory*, to them, and calling them his greatest mentors. And Shirley occasionally sings with her now-famous son. Check out the "Awake America" recording and video, which feature Shirley belting out the classic "My God Is Real" while Lindell and a group of top-notch studio musicians grind out a simmering gospel-blues accompaniment.

Perhaps surprisingly, Cooley is not smug or self-righteous about his peerless pentecostal pedigree or his coziness with God. He believes his life contains "a pattern of divine appointments," and he is deadly earnest about fulfilling the destiny he believes God has placed on him. But he does not take himself all that seriously, at times treating himself and his superspiritual background with a self-deprecating humor. For example, his book is full of numerous accounts of his weeping before the Lord, at times lying on his back and crying for hours until his hair is sopping wet. But today he can also laugh about such experiences. "Growing up pentecostal, we had a lot to cry about," he says over lunch at an Italian restaurant. "Everything was a sin, except eating."

One day during Cooley's teens, God gave him a strange vision of a contraption he says he had never seen before. Later, when he learned that the mysterious device was a mixing console, Cooley bought one and began making recordings of his and other people's music in his tiny bedroom.

Next, he toured with pentecostal singing sensation Rusty

Goodman, a former member of The Happy Goodman Family, and composer of such songs as "I Wouldn't Take Nothing for My Journey Now." Touring with Goodman exposed Cooley to many Assemblies of God pastors who thought he might make an excellent music minister, including Brownsville's John Kilpatrick. But before coming to Brownsville a decade later, Cooley went to Nashville, where he got a crash course in the contemporary Christian music industry.

From 1992 to 1994 Cooley was music director at Christ Church, a thirty-six hundred-member pentecostal congregation in Nashville. The long hours, the many responsibilities, and Cooley's enthusiastic zeal quickly burned him out on the job.

Cooley resigned and tried to make a go of it as a freelance producer. He stayed busy, even if he did not get any of Music City's plum assignments. Still, he says he withered amidst the cynicism of the city's Christian music establishment, which included plenty of talented musicians but few mature Christians or balanced lives.

Looking back on this period, Cooley calls it his "dark era." He began to question his spiritual heritage. Comparing his Bible to the teachings of his father and other spiritual mentors, he came to the conclusion that he had absorbed much of what he calls "pentecostal tomfoolery." He began attending Nashville's stately St. Bartholomew's Episcopal Church, where he fell in love with the majesty of the high church liturgy, and saw it as a welcome alternative to the barrenness of much pentecostal and evangelical worship.

Evangelicals have a good understanding of how Jesus can be your best friend, as well as the message of grace. Pentecostals worship the Holy Spirit and celebrate the mysterious and the unexplainable. But the liturgical churches have a respect for God the Father that you can't find in other churches. And I longed to see the majesty and awesome power of God. I longed for stability that wasn't swayed by emotions or circumstances. I wanted to feel the bigness and holiness of God untainted by too much familiarity.

Cooley's dark days in Nashville did not extinguish his faith or shake his strong sense of personal destiny. "I knew I had had experiences with God when I was a boy that I couldn't explain away, no matter how cynical or analytical I became."

From One Worshiper to Another

Lindell Cooley was not at Brownsville Assembly of God on Father's Day 1995, the day revival broke out; he was in the Ukraine on a musical missions trip. But he has been at the revival services ever since, leading the church's worship team and its various choirs through a rousing repertoire of rollicking gospel songs, praise choruses, and hymns.

A consummate professional, Cooley effortlessly leads church musicians and thousands of worshipers through a dizzying progression of key changes, tempo changes, and mood changes. But don't you dare call what he does "a performance"!

"I really don't pay a lot of attention to the people," he confesses. "I just go out there as a worshiper myself."

As Cooley walks out of the room where he, evangelist Steve Hill, and pastor John Kilpatrick meet before services, and heads for his collection of keyboards and electronic devices just to the left of the huge altar area's pulpit, he is asking God for guidance. Cooley, who believes songs are a form of conversation from believers to their Creator, asks God to help him in selecting and pacing the evening's songs:

I say, "Lord, I want to worship You tonight. What do I need to say to You first? And then what do I need to say next?" I try to select things God will respond to, and I trust Him to minister.

And if things work out, the feelings and emotions I am experiencing are hopefully in tune with what the people are feeling.

On most nights, Cooley and crew mix fast and slow numbers, usually beginning with up-tempo favorites like Andrew Smith's "All Your Promises"; cruising through powerful ballads like "The Blood Medley," which features modern versions of "Nothing but the Blood of Jesus," "Are You Washed in the Blood?" and "Power in the Blood"; before ending up with slower, more meditative Vineyard numbers like "Draw Me Close," "Let Your Glory Fall," or Wesley's "O For a Thousand Tongues to Sing" (a hymn which, at least in this congregation—where people believe that the spiritual gifts God gave believers in the first century are still in operation today—is more than mere metaphor or symbolism).

Cooley fell in love with the Vineyard choruses when he visited the Toronto revival in 1995. And he has also written his own material, like the driving rocker, "Can You See the Lamb?" and the quiet ballad, "Jesus, Lover of My Soul." One of the revival's most popular numbers is Andy Park's "We Will Ride," the chorus of which has inspired a popular bumper sticker that reads: "Yes, Lord, we will ride with You."

But at Brownsville there is no such thing as an order of worship or a song list, and praise band members usually don't have a clue about which songs they will be playing each night. That all depends on how the Spirit leads Cooley, who also frequently preaches mini-sermons between the verses of a song. During "Jesus, Lover of My Soul," for example, he delivers the following ad lib in perfect rhythm and pitch:

He's better than a doctor. He's better than a psychiatrist. He's better than a lawyer. He's better than a surgeon. With just one word He can set you free tonight from everything that has held you captive for years. There is power in His name!

Such unplanned spontaneity would drive most church musicians crazy, but the people at Brownsville not only accept it, they believe it is the best way to worship a living God. As Cooley sees it, spontaneity is a necessary and natural alternative to the deadening ritual of many churches:

> I don't get up in the morning and say, "I need to talk to my wife this morning." Instead, it's a natural thing. I want to talk to her, and I want her to talk to me.
>
> It's the same thing with worship. Jesus is here with us. Through the music, I am trying to ask, "Is He comfortable here? Is He happy here?"

Cooley is certainly happy at Brownsville. During some services, he backs away from his keyboards, giving him more room to hop in the air and jump with glee, raising his eyes and his arms to heaven and losing himself in a joyful jig. At other times, he weeps as he sings, a visible outward symbol of his belief that true worship includes not only joy, but also sorrow, contrition, brokenness, and repentance. No one would mistake even these somber Brownsville moments for an Episcopal liturgy, but they are Cooley's attempt to capture the feeling of deep awe and reverence for God he believes liturgical worshipers experience with regularity, and which pumped-up pentecostals need to experience for themselves.

To the casual observer, it may seem that Cooley is a religious ringmaster, turning up the holy hype at one moment, then plunging the congregation into contemplation the next. But he says he does it all for God's pleasure, not for the people's reaction. "I know a lot of people who are capable of whipping a crowd into a frenzy, but that never goes anywhere," he says. "I despise that."

Behind the Scenes

Brownsville's busy schedule is enough to drive any music minister crazy. There is a long Sunday morning service, and then there are the nightly revival services, which are held Wednesday through Saturday and can last until the wee hours of the morning. There is a 150-voice church choir, a youth choir that's just as big, and a variety of soloists, ensembles, and bands.

Cooley is thankful he does not have to do everything himself, and he delegates responsibility for many of the music department's rehearsals and details to assistants. In fact, before he ever agreed to come to Brownsville, he made Pastor John Kilpatrick agree to a detailed list of twenty-nine demands that guarantee Cooley time to be with his family and freedom from keeping strict office hours.

But Cooley is the glue that holds Brownsville's music ministry together. And even though he is a perfectionist at heart, the only time he demands the absolute best from his people is when they are making a record. "People in the church who aren't musicians can tell when I'm recording," he says. "They tell me the music (in the services) doesn't flow at those times."

The rest of the time, Cooley's approach is more laid back: "You rehearse, you rehearse, and you rehearse. You get it as right as you can. And when you get into the sanctuary, you forget about all that and relax."

In the past, revival song leaders like Homer Rodeheaver have created manuals and conferences to teach their techniques to other music leaders. Today, teaching other music ministers to loosen up and liven up is one of the goals for the worship leaders' conferences Cooley organizes. Around a thousand people attended the first conference in 1998, and a second is scheduled for spring 1999. Cooley says:

A lot of the time, worship leaders get so caught up in the arrangements that they forget about worship. I'm trying to get these guys off of their lists, out of their books, and loosen them up to play what God has given them.

Cooley has also created his own company, Music Missions International, which sells tapes, CDs, videos, songbooks, and other materials. The company's profits are used to fund further overseas musical missionary trips. "The last thing the world needs is another worship record or another worship leader. We've got enough, thank you. But if we can help churches elsewhere in the world, that's a worthwhile thing."

Just by virtue of being the worship leader of the Brownsville revival, Cooley has become famous, playing his music for more people than all but the most popular of contemporary Christian artists. He is wary of the pride that can pollute a person who makes the slow and subtle transition from worshiping God for revival to believing that he himself is responsible for it.

Pride is a snare that has trapped previous song leaders. Charles Alexander, for example, infuriated evangelist R. A. Torrey when the musician started bringing his own publicist along on crusades. And Rodeheaver distributed promotional literature in which he was hailed as "the world's greatest song leader."

"Musicians seem to have an old link to Lucifer, the first rebellious worship leader," says Cooley. "They have a pride that is never satisfied."

But Cooley, who in his day has seen a fair number of pentecostal revivals flare up and die away, knows that the forces that have brought him renown will some day return him to the relative anonymity he prefers. "This revival will end," he says matter-of-factly.

While he finds some of the Brownsville revival furor exciting, he also finds much of it draining. Standing during the long hours of revival services has given him a bad case of varicose veins. He will keep giving his all as long as he believes God keeps appearing, but when that's not the case any more, he will be glad to get back to church as usual.

> The ride up is really fun, but the ride down the other side is different. Something like this may never happen to other (musicians) on the same level, or they may do more. But that's not the point.
>
> My purpose—and everyone's purpose—is to fulfill our destiny. God is busy working out the character of Christ in us all. And I find happiness in that, not in who I am or what I'm doing. It's about who *He* is.

Making Beautiful Music Together

So what can churches do to care for and nurture their worship leaders? Cooley offers these ideas.

Remember: It's a Calling, Not a Job

Just as Steve Hill questions the wisdom of pastors who try to preach without passion, Cooley is skeptical about worship leaders who view what they do more as work than as worship.

Put another way, the message could be: You're about praise, not performance.

Too often music that is borne of a powerful spiritual awakening becomes dull and boring through thoughtless and emotionless execution. That happened with long-established gospel songs created in earlier revivals, and it has even happened in churches that sing praise and worship music developed during the Jesus movement and in the Vineyard churches. If you have ever visited a church where potentially moving songs are executed with great professionalism but little spiritual sensitivity, you know the problem. Instead of churning out more "praise products" for popular consumption, focus on the act of praise itself, and see if people in your congregation don't participate with passion.

Pursue Excellence, Then Relax

Cooley believes that God appreciates excellence. He drives the members of the Brownsville worship team hard. When they're learning new material, he practices difficult passages ad nauseam, and does everything he can to get them right.

But when it comes time to worship, he adapts to a different paradigm. It's no longer hard work and discipline; instead it's taking what you've got and offering it up to God as a gift to Him and as a sacrifice for Him to accept.

Of course, some church musicians never get their material to a polished level to begin with, and that's a serious problem. But the point is, when it comes time to worship, it's no longer time to be practicing parts and focusing on musical minutiae. It's time to meet God and to help others do the same.

Love Your Worship Leader

Churches often want conflicting qualities from their worship leaders. On the one hand, they want creative, artistic types who can create mystical music that moves the flock. On the other hand, they want punch-the-clock bureaucratic types who will put in standard office hours, manage a church music department, and work horrendous hours with a smile. Few humans can handle both roles well.

Such treatment should be forbidden for church staff anyway, but perhaps worship leaders have their own unique reasons for getting special treatment. After all, their job is to inspire others. That is difficult when they are overwhelmed themselves. And the requirement to hold office hours should take into consideration the hours musicians spend in rehearsals, evaluating new music, and keeping their skills in shape.

But beyond that, more churches need to treat their worship leaders with the type of respect Hill and Kilpatrick give Cooley: as a spiritual equal and a co-laborer in the revival. They show admiration and respect for his work. They lavish him with affection. They honor his sense of calling and his innate feel for God's will and direction. And they let him control much of the flow of the revival services, instead of merely asking him to fill brief gaps in the program with music. Who wouldn't want to work and serve God in such an environment?

Changed Lives

"God spoke to my heart"

Jon Beedham thought of God as a cosmic Santa Claus until the preaching at Brownsville struck his heart.

Help for a Good Kid

During revival it is often the sensational night-and-day conversions of big-time sinners that get all the attention. But Jon Beedham's renewal has been just as dramatic, even though, as he says, "I was a good kid."

"I never went to church. My mom was a New Age Buddhist.

My stepdad was like a backslider. I didn't know anything about Jesus. I thought He was a guy who lived two thousand years ago. I knew there was a God, but I looked at God like a big Santa Claus. I wasn't looking for that."

But things changed after stepdad Juan Moreno went to revival services at Brownsville. "He came to the revival, and God totally changed his life and turned him around," says Jon. "Then he made the whole family go to church." Soon Jon's mom, Jean, and his five-year-old sister, Miranda, gave their lives to God. "Miranda has had some visions of God, Jesus, and angels. She's getting touched. I believe she's going to grow up to be a woman of God."

Before Brownsville, Jon had only been to church a few times in his thirteen years. And each time, the result was total boredom.

"But when I went to Brownsville and heard Steve Hill and his preaching—he preaches hard—God spoke to my heart. He showed me I was a sinner, that I had broken His laws, and that He has a divine plan for me."

Unlike many who have been touched by God during the revival, Jon says he never shook or convulsed. "I think the reason God shakes people is to get out the filth that had been built up over the years," he says. "I didn't have a lot of filth, so God didn't have to do that to me."

Still, getting saved at the revival has made a big difference in Jon's life. "Ever since then, people say they know I found Jesus. But I didn't find Jesus; He found me."

The whole purpose of Jon's life has changed, from thinking only of himself to serving God and others.

"Whenever I prayed, I asked for stuff. I never sought God. I never worshiped Him and praised Him. Now, that's all I want to do."

For Jon, the day starts early—about 5:15 A.M.—when he hops out of bed to pray. "I'm pretty zoned out at that time in the morning, but I cannot go through a day without talking to God first and putting it in His hands. It's a battle. There are so many people who don't know Jesus, and there are so many demonic things in the world. I've got to get ready."

He arrives early at high school, where he and a group of other students meet in the school lobby for prayer. There is also a school Bible club on Tuesdays, and a big Brownsville youth service on Thursday nights.

"It's all just a movement toward God and going after Him, forsaking yourself, your own desires, your own wants, and just going after Him and not living for yourself any more," says Jon.

Even though Jon was not saved from a life of horrible sin and unhappiness, he is still grateful for what the revival has done for him. And he is convinced that God holds the key to wholeness for the other members of his generation.

"For teenagers today, there are so many temptations out there, and so many things the devil wants us to do. He wants to have this generation, but I believe God is raising this generation up. He is showing them that He is in control, that He loves them, and that He has a plan for them."

At first skeptical about revival, youth minister Richard Crisco now demands that his kids demonstrate their zeal through holy, disciplined lives.

CHAPTER SEVEN

Your Young Shall See Visions:

Youth Minister Richard Crisco

What would you do if your church were suddenly hit by a blazing fire, destroying church structures and causing the cancellation of long-cherished programs? In a very real sense, that's what happened after revival broke out at Brownsville Assembly of God.

Fire, as in Holy Ghost revival fire, hit the church, and overnight the once-conservative church was transformed into revival central. Nearly everything on the church's usually packed schedule of activities was canceled to clear the way for the move of God in revival services, services that have now lasted for more than three years.

Among those thrown into chaos by the whole affair was Brownsville's youth minister, Richard Crisco, a convert from Catholicism whose years in the Assemblies of God had done little to prepare him for the intense spiritual fervor that now surrounded him.

At first Crisco was skeptical about the emotionalism of the revival. He worried that in the hothouse atmosphere of spiritual awakening, believers would begin substituting experiences for discipleship, feelings for the fundamentals of the faith. "I don't care if people shake, or fall, or speak in tongues," he says. "I want to see a difference in their lives."

But soon enough, Crisco was seeing plentiful evidence of

transformed lives all around him. As he says, some of the brats and snots he had struggled with for years became saints and angels. Kids who had been lukewarm or worse began to be on fire for God. Bickering and petty rivalries disappeared, replaced by a deep hunger for things of the Spirit. Instead of demanding that the group organize parties and recreational activities, young people began spending their evenings and weekends in lengthy prayer sessions.

"I got saved in revival and my whole lifestyle has changed," says sixteen-year-old Sara. "If you want to sin you can't, because you have so many people around you to keep you accountable." Robin says she has been transformed too. "Revival totally changed the way I see life."

It was as if the Old Testament prophecy of Joel were being powerfully fulfilled:

And it shall come to pass afterward
That I will pour out My Spirit on all flesh;
Your sons and your daughters shall prophesy . . .
Your young men shall see visions.
(2:28)

As attendance at youth group meetings soared from a pre-revival average of around a hundred to a post-revival average of more than four hundred, and around seven hundred kids turned out for weekly youth services, Crisco made a bold move: he upped the ante on his kids, creating a demanding new program that requires youngsters to keep logs of their prayer life, their efforts at witnessing to others about their faith, and the time they spend in studying the Bible.

Crisco calls it the Master's Plan Discipleship Program, and it is based on his two ministry foundations: the Great Commandment (love God with all your heart, and love your neighbor as yourself) and the Great Commission (take the gospel into all the world). He says the program, which encourages kids both to go deeper with God and to take their faith out into the world, is "so simple it's embarrassing."

Still, about three hundred youth group members at Brownsville are making its disciplines a part of their daily lives. And after he began making it available to other youth groups in mid-1996, hundreds of churches adopted it. "I had no idea this was something we would share with anybody else," he says, "but now I hear that hundreds of thousands of young people are using it."

The revival at Brownsville and the success of the Master's Plan Discipleship Program has done more than radically change one congregation and its youth program. It has given Richard Crisco a national platform, and he is using that platform to give other youth workers the message that today's kids want more from their churches than pizza parties and fun. They want a transforming, life-changing relationship with the living God.

"We've made a major mistake," says Crisco, who organized Brownsville's first annual youth conference in July 1997. "We've built our youth programs around entertainment, and as a result we've built youth groups instead of youth ministries." And for now, he's doing everything he can to change that.

Not a Priest, but a Preacher

Richard Crisco, who was raised in Milton, Florida, just a stone's throw away from Brownsville, grew up in a solidly Catholic family, which included a catechesis-teaching mother and a variety of great aunts and uncles who were nuns and priests. When his grandmother Mimi was on her deathbed, she pressured Richard, then in the sixth grade, to say that he, too, would be a priest when he grew up.

But it was not to be. Crisco fell in love with a pretty young Assemblies of God girl, and the only way her daddy would let him date her was if he agreed to attend church with her. For more than two years Crisco dutifully attended morning services with his family at St. Rose of Lima Catholic Church before going to evening church with his girlfriend at Holt Assembly of God.

"I received the Lord there one Sunday night," recalls Crisco, who says his Catholic upbringing gave him a deep respect for God and a good understanding of Christian teaching, but failed to teach him about one crucial piece of the puzzle—the necessity of a personal relationship with the living Christ.

A couple of years later, Crisco was up late one night working on his finance homework for a class at Pensacola Junior College when God spoke to him about entering the ministry. "He said, 'It's now time.' I knew the Lord had called me to the ministry. I knew that I knew that I knew. But now I had to do one of the hardest things I had ever done in my life: telling my parents."

His mom and dad took it better than grandmother Mimi might have. In fact, Crisco says both have made deeper commitments to the Lord and have visited their son at Brownsville. "They've been very supportive," he says.

Giving a Father's Love

The Brownsville revival has made international religious superstars out of evangelist Steve Hill, pastor John Kilpatrick, and worship leader Lindell Cooley. It has also given newfound notoriety to Crisco, although he has been loath to hop on the bandwagon, preferring instead to keep a relatively low profile. "I feel unworthy of the attention I've been given," he says.

Crisco routinely turns down most of the hundreds of speaking requests he gets, agreeing to only one out-of-town engagement per month. Home is where his heart is, and that means focusing on his wife and two children as well as devoting himself to the hundreds of Brownsville kids who look up to him as a kind of surrogate father. "I get more joy and satisfaction out of our Thursday night youth services than I would out of going national. I'm trying to keep my mind on what's truly successful, and what's truly important."

For Crisco, the most important thing is giving his kids a stable and steadfast love that is often at odds with the emotional confusion, instability, and outright rejection they experience elsewhere in their lives. "Young people need the security of knowing you will be there," he says.

Talk to Crisco for any time at all, or visit one of the youth ministry classes he teaches at the Brownsville Revival School of Ministry, and there is one word you will hear him repeat over and over. That word is *love*.

His whole philosophy of youth ministry can be boiled down to one simple equation: Love God and love kids. "This generation is so hungry for love," he tells future youth ministers. "Don't be afraid to express your love to your people."

Of course, he is very cautious and deliberate about the manner in which he demonstrates his affection. "We've got to be careful about the expression of that love," he says. Periodically he brings his wife, Jane, into youth services for a refresher course on hugging. "This is how I hug my wife," he says, pulling her closer to him until the two are face-to-face in a tight embrace. "And this is how I hug my girls," he says, picking a high school student out of the group, standing next to her, and putting one arm around her shoulders. During the frequent times he hugs the guys in the group, he intentionally gives them the same kind of tight embrace he gives his wife, and he makes sure it lasts longer than the hugs with the girls. Not only is he trying to soften up some of his macho young men, but he is also trying to demonstrate to both males and females that it is important to exercise sexual control as well as practice a heightened sensitivity to sexual "vibes."

Crisco is even more careful about anyone else who wants to express love to his kids. Adult sponsors who volunteer to work with the church's young people must fill out a four-page application, provide three personal references, have their fingerprints taken, and submit to a criminal background check.

Within these firm and inviolable boundaries, however, Crisco is extremely loving and expressive. And his kids love him for it, many of them calling him "Papa Ricky."

"It's like he's my dad," says youth group member Sara. "I live with my mom and my brother, so Richard is like a father figure to me." Eric, a high school junior, says, "He's just an average guy, but it's his vision to be like Jesus that makes him extraordinary."

Love Must Also Be Tough

Not everything is hugs and happiness. Crisco follows the admonitions of his hero, James Dobson, founder of Focus on the Family and author of the best-selling 1983 book, *Love Must Be Tough*. "The stronger the relationship I have with my kids," says Crisco, "the harder I can come down on them."

Crisco practices strict discipline, expelling kids who show no interest in spiritual growth. "If you want to go for God, then you are in the right place," he tells his kids. "But if you have come here to goof around, then you are out of here." If he does kick a kid out, he follows up with a phone call to clarify that it was the youngster's behavior—not any personal animosity—that caused the problem.

Crisco's tough-and-tender approach toward discipline comes not only from listening to Dobson but from his study of the life of Christ. In Luke 19 Jesus drove the money changers out of the temple in Jerusalem, telling them, "It is written, 'My house is a house of prayer,' but you have made it a den of thieves" (v. 46). But four verses earlier, Jesus had wept over the city of Jerusalem as He approached it from a distance.

"Never whip the people until you have wept over the people," says Crisco. "You cannot preach hard unless the people know you love them."

Crisco weeps for his kids. He regularly looks at their photos, which he keeps in big, bulging photo albums in a shelf behind his desk. He spends hours of "carpet time," lying on the floor and praying to God for their well-being. And he writes plentiful personal notes and makes numerous phone calls, all in an effort to express his love for them. But when it comes time for that love to be tough, Crisco does not shirk his responsibility.

As he tells his youth ministry students, motivating young people requires the following four-step process:

1. Respect. "Everyone deserves an element of respect," he says. "And Philippians 2:3 tells us, 'in lowliness of mind let each esteem others better than himself.' I have learned that if you respect others, they will eventually learn to respect you."

2. Relationship. "Our ability to motivate our youth will increase drastically when we can develop relationships with our teens."

3. Recognize and reward. Quoting another of his guiding lights, Crisco says, "John Maxwell teaches the principle, 'What gets rewarded gets done.' I try to put this into practice by pulling a couple of my teens who are fulfilling the goals of our vision onto the platform with me to recognize them. I try never to reward negative behavior, only positive attitudes and actions."

4. Revelation. "Our ultimate goal as pastors is to bring teens into contact with our Mighty God and allow Him to burn a revelation into their spirit. When they catch a vision for God, you will no longer have to worry about them constantly falling into the snares of sin."

Still, Crisco believes all his efforts to show love to his kids would be worthless without an equally strong effort to foster his own love for God.

"Programs without the love of God are just diddly squat," he tells his youth ministry class, edging about as close as he will ever get to swearing or using coarse language. "The greatest thing you can do for your teens is to become a man or a woman of God."

Then Crisco steps from behind his lectern and begins pacing

the floor and looking his youth ministry students directly in their eyes. "You teach what you know, but you reproduce what you are. Your kids will ultimately end up being like you.

"If you've been a youth pastor at a church for three years and your kids are hopping into bed with each other, I suggest you take a look at your lust life. If you've been there three years and your kids are having a problem with gossip and backbiting, I suggest you take a hard look at the things you're saying about people behind their backs. You teach what you know, but you reproduce what you are."

Programmed for Powerful Living

Richard Crisco is trying to reproduce die-hard disciples with his Master's Plan Discipleship Program. He readily admits there is nothing magical about his method: it simply translates lofty and sometimes ambiguous ideals like spiritual growth into specific tasks that kids can do each day. He also readily admits there is nothing original about the program, which is based on Student Discipleship Ministries' daily devotional guide for young people.

"I've taken their approach and added to it my own list of Bible readings, so that every day our kids are reading a chapter from the Old Testament, a chapter from the New Testament, and a chapter from the book of Proverbs, plus memorizing key Bible verses every week," says Crisco. "In addition, there are a series of activity sheets that help the kids keep track of various things. There is a daily prayer journal. There's a sheet for keeping track of a person they witness to each week. There's a check-off for fasting one meal per week. And there are places for notes on all the sermons and messages they hear."

Crisco knows that such a program could be deadly drudgery if not balanced with a real spiritual vitality. But when he designed the program, it was not his kids' vitality he was worried about. Instead, he was concerned about how grounded they were in the foundations of the faith.

In the midst of all my feelings when revival broke out was intense fear. Everyone else was excited, but I was scared. I saw potential for trouble. I knew that I could end up with a bunch of shallow, emotional teenagers who were merely living off of the experience.

So this is what I say to my young people: "When the devil comes and tempts you—and he will—what are you going to do? Will you start to shake and expect him to run? Are you going to 'fall in the Spirit' and play dead and think the devil is going to leave you alone? No! You will have to do exactly what Jesus did! Pick up the Word of God and say, "It is written. It is written. It is written!"

As tough as the Master's Plan Discipleship Program is, there are a few dozen youth at the church for whom even it is not tough enough. For these hardy young souls, Crisco has developed something he calls the Ultimate Training Core. Young people who want to be involved in leadership in Brownsville's youth programs must complete both the Master's Plan program and the Ultimate Training Core. The purpose of the UTC is "to produce heavily armed warriors that will not be shaken by the quakes of the dark side . . . The world has been witnesses of 'casual Christianity' long enough. It is time for a group to rise far and beyond that which is expected of them."

The UTC program is run by two young people Crisco has been discipling for years: twenty-one-year-old Mike Wood and twenty-year-old Ruth Moore. Every Sunday morning for ten weeks, Wood and Moore run their charges through a grueling course, which includes sessions on leadership training, lesson plan development, and personal spiritual growth. In addition to the Master Plan requirements, those youth taking the UTC course must commit to a daily quiet time and thirty minutes of daily intercessory prayer for others.

"The leader is not going to bicker because he has a minimum requirement," says Mike Wood, issuing a challenge to the kids.

"If he is required to pray for thirty minutes, he's going to pray for forty. He's going to go far and beyond."

The UTC course also contains something called the Thorn in the Flesh. This consists of a series of hard questions the UTC youth must answer, such as:

- "Am I closer to the Lord today than I was yesterday?"
- "Have you been in or allowed yourself to be in an inappropriate situation this week?"

Leader Ruth Moore says such questions do not constitute badgering, they merely help along the way. "You are not ordinary youth," she says. "There's a higher calling on you, and it's time to step up to it. We're not asking you to do anything we're not doing ourselves."

History Makers

Throughout the history of the church, those awakenings that have had the greatest impact have usually harnessed the energy and idealism of youth.

Jonathan Edwards, in his firsthand account of First Great Awakening, *A Narrative of Surprising Conversions*, describes the ways in which that historic revival impacted his community of Northampton in contrasting "before" and "after" portraits. First, the "before":

> Licentiousness for some years prevailed among youth of the town; they were many of them very much addicted to night-walking, and frequenting the tavern, and lewd practices, wherein some, by their example, exceedingly corrupted others.

And then, the "after":

Those who were formerly loose young persons are generally, to all appearance, become true lovers of God and Christ, and spiritual in their dispositions.

Similar "before" and "after" portraits could be painted of many of the Brownsville young people, some of whom were previously excited about anything but the Christian life. Now they are deeply devoted to God and using their lives to serve Him.

Edwards would certainly be impressed with the Brownsville teens' bold stand on sexual purity. Crisco is an outspoken critic of the American approach toward dating, which he calls "a lie from the pit of hell." Not only does dating sometimes destroy church youth groups, he also believes it presents young people with sexual temptations that are too enticing to resist. He tells his kids to save their bodies and their hearts for one person—their future lifelong partner. And more than 250 of his kids have signed a pledge that is intended to help them do just that.

This pledge is a courtship covenant that kids enter into with their parents. The covenant basically does away with dating, which is designed to allow kids to play the field, in exchange for courtship, which is designed to focus on finding a suitable mate. Kids who sign the pledge agree to submit to their parents' guidance in finding them a suitable marriage partner. "Next to giving their lives to Jesus, the most important decision young people make is who they spend their future with," says Crisco.

Clearly, some of the biggest impact Brownsville youth have had in their community has been in area schools, but according to local school officials, not all of it has been good. On numerous occasions, school administrators in the Pensacola area have been forced to phone Crisco and others at Brownsville for immediate help in solving a pressing problem: some of their students who regularly attend the revival occasionally break out in "attacks" of shaking and jerking. When calls like these come in, Crisco drops everything and rushes to the schools, where he tries to calm both enraptured students and incomprehensible officials.

Crisco, however, is more excited to discuss other ways his kids' newfound zeal is having an impact on local schools. For example, he says that prior to revival, Brownsville students were involved in Bible clubs and other student-led ministries at only three local schools. Today Brownsville youth are leading or involved in activities at more than thirty area schools. "We are now part of campus ministries at every college, university, junior college, high school, and junior high school in this area," he says.

Or, as he tells his kids: "We don't live to feel God, we live to serve Him regardless. I have watched you shake and tremble and cry. Now I want you to shake your schools."

Crisco's continual challenging of his kids, as well as his solid stance against dating, show that he does not mind swimming against the cultural tide. And his approach to pop culture shows that sometimes he does not mind getting out of the water altogether.

"If someone came up to me and put a gun to my head and told me to name one movie in the theaters today, I'd say 'Pull the trigger,'" he says. "The same thing goes for rock music. I couldn't name two rock groups who have albums out right now." Crisco says he is not advocating ignorance about the broader culture, but when pressed, he says he would rather be ignorant of it than immersed in it. "If I had to go one way or the other, that's the way I would go."

Hope for a Generation

History teaches that we should not underestimate what one lowly church worker can do to inspire and inflame kids. After all, Dwight Moody was brought to Christ by his Sunday school teacher, and then Moody, the leading evangelist of his era, went on to bring thousands more to Christ himself.

That's not all. Moody also helped found the Student Volunteer Movement for Foreign Missions, which was designed to encourage young people to devote their lives to spreading the gospel. As this movement spread across the country and around the world, more than one thousand youth signed a pledge that read, "It is my purpose, if God permit, to become a foreign missionary."

At times, Richard Crisco feels a little like a modern-day Moody. He does not know how far some of his kids will go, but he is convinced that many of them will wind up devoting their lives to God's service. By insisting that Christianity can be more than a consumer religion, and that youth ministry can be more than pizza parties, he has bucked youth ministry conventions.

But perhaps his biggest point of departure with conventional wisdom is his no-holds-barred belief in the powerful potential of the current generation of youth, which he has nicknamed The Elisha Generation. Unlike those who dismiss today's teens as too self-centered to get involved in the world's problems, or too insensitive to care, Crisco finds today's youth full of passion and conviction. As he writes in his book, *It's Time*:

> In some ways this is the most abused, neglected, and misunderstood generation in the history of mankind. This generation understands pain. They have experienced it. That is why some of them experience God's love in such a powerful way. And it's why some of them can become so involved in intercessory prayer and travailing for other people's pain.
>
> But more than that, this generation has a deep and powerful hunger for God. This generation doesn't want to come to religious services. They want to come to a place where God is.

Janet, one of the teens in Crisco's group, agrees. "Teenagers are sick of religion," she says. "We're sick of going to church and leaving the same way we came every Sunday. We are hungry for God; and we're hungry for His power."

Crisco is doing everything he can do to fill that hunger with the foundational truths of the Christian faith and the living power of the Holy Spirit. As he told me:

> This generation doesn't have a sin problem, they have a vision problem. They are looking for a purpose. They are looking for a cause to die for. If more of us would quit focusing on "youth groups" and begin focusing on "youth ministry," we could help them discover their purpose and their ministry.

That's the message Crisco will keep delivering for as long as revival continues at Brownsville, even after the fires calm down and the spotlights are turned off.

> I've always been satisfied being a nobody, and I'll be satisfied going back to being a nobody. I don't really care what happens. I'm just going to continue pouring my life into my young people. I can change the world more this way than I can by traveling around the world and making a name for myself.

Going for the Gusto

You don't have to wait for revival to transform your church before you can start transforming your church's youth ministry. No matter what happens, you can begin taking a few of the following steps to motivate and minister to your young people.

Set a Higher Standard

Which would you rather do: set a low standard that every kid can easily meet; or set a higher standard that forces everyone to push a little harder? Many youth ministries choose the former, fearful that if they emphasize the latter they will face criticism or lose attendance.

Richard Crisco's experience at Brownsville shows that

tougher can be better. Kids there respond to programs that force them to get serious about God. Perhaps your group can be an island of spiritual depth and moral excellence in a world that is lost and drowning in mediocrity.

Model Disciplined, Consistent Love

Kids today are bombarded by all the wrong kinds of sex. Prime-time TV sitcoms major on lust but are silent about love. Movies and videos feature much more skin than they do imagination, plot, or character development. Even the president of the United States has found himself in sexual scandals that had school kids across the nation discussing oral sex.

One thing few kids ever get a chance to see, however, is what healthy and affectionate love looks like. They are hungry for affection, but often that hunger has wound up leading them into pain, not purity. Make your youth group a place where affection can be expressed freely in a sensitive and disciplined way. And make sure that you give your kids the kind of consistent and steadfast affection they need.

Connect Kids to God

Too often youth groups do tons of good things without doing the best thing. Games can be great. Field trips can be fun. Camping trips or concerts can be cool. But introducing a young person to the love and guidance of God Almighty is in a category all its own.

If creating disciples is your number-one goal, what are your programs and activities doing to promote that goal? Take a hard look at the way you plan your group's activities. Throw out things that do not promote young people's long-term spiritual development, and focus more on helping them understand and live out their faith.

Changed Lives

A pied piper?
*Public school administrator Chip Woolwine (with
hand raised) ran into trouble when he invited kids
to the revival.*

Revived and Removed

Chip Woolwine had been an award-winning teacher and popular administrator in northwest Florida's Okaloosa County
School District for twenty years. He spent nine of those twenty
years at Niceville High School, the last three as vice-principal.

As for his devout faith in Jesus Christ, Woolwine was an "open book." He was the sponsor of Niceville's student-initiated Bible Study Club. Three times he gladly accepted invitations to speak at off-campus evening meetings of the school's growing chapter of the Fellowship of Christian Athletes program. In addition, he and his wife, Rosemary, hosted a Monday-evening Bible study for teens in their home.

In August 1995 Woolwine attended a revival service at Brownsville Assembly of God. "I liked it," he recalls. "I enjoyed the music and the preaching, but I left with no particular intention of returning."

But he did return, and by his third visit he realized that he had been changed. Soon, revival touched his tenth-grade son, Zack, and eight-grade daughter, Chelsea.

Back at work, Woolwine had a new boldness to share his faith. "I had a deep desire to see students discover the peace, joy, and freedom that accompany a saving relationship with Jesus," he says. "Niceville High School, which stood in the shadow of an awesome move of God, began to experience firsthand the inevitable and undeniable impact of revival."

Friends say Woolwine had a fresh "anointing" to share his faith. Students often came to him with their problems, and he occasionally suggested biblical solutions. In addition, in his free time he accompanied dozens of students to revival services.

After a group of students approached Woolwine and Jack Wilson, a Niceville science teacher and FCA sponsor, asking the men to baptize the students in a local bayou, Woolwine says he checked with the school principal, who told him to secure signed parental consent forms. Approximately ten students were baptized at a moving service attended by nearly one hundred parents, family members, and friends.

"Students were getting saved, baptized, and delivered from life-controlling problems such as alcohol abuse, drug abuse, lust, inappropriate sexual behavior, bondage to memories of sexual abuse, low self-esteem, thoughts of suicide, and a host of other awful situations," says Woolwine.

"There was a move of the Lord that swept through our student body. And as this happened, we began to see school discipline improve. When these kids were saved by Jesus, repented of their sins, and experienced the impact of the Holy Spirit, their lives began to change in very positive ways."

Soon some parents, school board members, and local church officials began to express disapproval of Woolwine and Wilson's activities. One couple, for example, was shocked when their sixteen-year-old daughter said her uncontrollable shaking was caused by the Holy Spirit. Others began calling Woolwine "the pied piper of Brownsville." He felt he had become the subject of a modern-day witch hunt.

On June 23, 1997, at an emotionally charged school board meeting, Woolwine and Wilson were disciplined for violating policies requiring school employees to remain "neutral" with regard to religion. Woolwine was suspended without pay for five days, placed on a one-year period of probation, and permanently transferred to a position within the district where he would have no further student contact.

Woolwine was shocked. "If you ask me if I believe I am guilty of doing something wrong, I would say 'no.' If you ask me if I believe I am guilty of violating school board policy, I would say 'no.' But if you ask me if I believe I am guilty of violating someone's interpretation of school board policy, then I would say 'yes.' After all, the school board voted against me five-to-zero."

He did not fare much better with a conservative Christian organization that pledged to help him.

On October 9, 1997, a segment about the Woolwine controversy was broadcast on Pat Robertson's *700 Club* TV program. To Robertson, the episode was another chilling example of the erosion of religious liberties. Robertson said American courts were behind a "squeeze" on believers' freedoms, which was similar to what had happened to the "Jews in Nazi Germany." And he promised that the American Center for Law and Justice—a group founded by Robertson for the purpose of battling liberalism and the ACLU and headed by attorney Jay Sekulow—would take up Woolwine's plight and fight the school board. As Robertson stated during *The 700 Club* broadcast:

> They're going to get sued by the ACLJ. We're gonna ask for damages, and it's going to be a big hassle, and we're going to take it all the way to the Supreme Court, and they're going to be in litigation for the next four or five years because we're not going to let that principal be abused that way.

But Robertson failed to deliver on his promise. The ACLJ did broker a settlement agreement, but both Woolwine and Wilson considered it weak and compromising, and declined to sign it. Shortly thereafter, the ACLJ withdrew as the men's counsel.

Woolwine says he finds the whole episode "interesting," but does not regret sharing his faith in Jesus with the students. When the ABC news program *20/20* asked him what, if anything, he would do differently, his response was quick and clear: "Nothing! To save my job, to save my career—which one of the students would I send back to the awful life that they were experiencing? The answer is I wouldn't send any of them back."

Michael Brown has plenty of impressive-sounding credentials, but his brain doesn't keep his heart from worshiping with abandon.

CHAPTER EIGHT

Preparing Laborers for the Harvest:

Michael Brown and the Brownsville Revival School of Ministry

Students at the Brownsville Revival School of Ministry do not need physical education classes. They have chapel.

Every Tuesday more than a thousand students—nearly all of them converted or transformed through revival services at the nearby Brownsville Assembly of God—start their school day with a rousing, rocking, no-holds-barred time of singing, dancing, and worshiping.

"I feel like praising Him," sing the students, propelled by the pulsating beat of a high-decibel praise band whose members, most of whom have no background in the Assemblies denomination, lean more toward contemporary Christian music's pop- and rock-oriented sound than they do toward the church's southern gospel-flavored worship.

"I feel like clapping my hands," they sing, punctuating their praise with energetic applause.

"I feel like shouting for joy," they sing, nearly raising the roof of the auditorium with a deafening roar before heading into the heartfelt chorus closer:

"I could dance, dance, dance, dance, dance all night long."

A good portion of the students twirl, hop, jump, or move to the beat, showing that dancing to the Lord is not merely a topic that comes up during a study of King David. These kids dance as an all-out act of devotion to God, and they do so with all the energy of a Sufi whirling dervish, or a chanting Hare Krishna devotee, or even a slam-dancing, mosh-pit-diving, rock-and-rolling concert-goer, which is precisely what some of them were none too long ago, before their path led them to Pensacola and the life-changing power of God.

"We've got people who have been out of school for twenty years, people who just got their GEDs, and people with master's degrees, and even medical doctors," says Michael Brown, who has been the school's president since it opened its doors in January 1997. "We have people who one year ago were drug addicts or strippers. Others have been in the ministry for years. We've got the whole range. But what they all have in common is a tremendous hunger for God and a tremendous desire to see the world saved, no matter what the cost."

Brown dances and hops with nearly as much enthusiasm as some of his students, putting his lanky, six-foot-three frame through a crash course in Christian calisthenics, which severely tests nearly every seam in his traditional-looking black suit.

Brown, a former Conservative Jew who met Jesus during his turbulent teen years, is as fervent in his praise as any forty-three year old could be, but his energy does not match that of his students, many of whom still bask in the amazing grace of their recent spiritual awakenings, and most of whom have left jobs, family, and friends to come to Pensacola, where they pray, study, and seek to understand how God may want to use their lives.

Some want to be preachers. Others are preparing to become missionaries. And some are not quite sure what they will wind up doing, saying, "I will serve Him in whatever way He wants to use me." Undoubtedly, there are challenges ahead for some of these students as they struggle to translate their overwhelming zeal into ministries and careers. But for now, as they are worshiping with utter abandon, only a few students are struck by the flailing hands of fellow worshipers, and none are seriously hurt.

When the singing stops and Brown steps to the pulpit to begin a time of prayer, a deafening hush falls upon the room. All one can hear is students fanning themselves, or trying to catch their breath. "Lord, let Your name be exalted," says Brown, to a chorus of hearty groans and amens. "May we be a holy avalanche. May the momentum be unstoppable."

Balancing Mind and Heart

Most of the time, Brown prays in English; but not always. Occasionally, he rises to lead his students in prayer, and what comes out sounds something like this: *Yivarekaka vieshmaraka.*

Like others at the school, Brown believes that the whole range of spiritual gifts bestowed upon the first Christians by the Holy Spirit are still operative today. But this time he was not speaking or praying in tongues. Instead, he was reciting—in Hebrew—one of the priestly prayers found in the Old Testament book of Numbers; in English it means, "The Lord bless you and keep you."

Hebrew is just one of the fifteen or so ancient languages that Brown, who holds a Ph.D. in Near Eastern Languages and Literatures from New York University, can speak or read. He works with Greek and Aramaic, as well as Akkadian, Ugaritic, Syriac, Phoenician, Punic, and Moabite, along with German and Yiddish.

He has written nearly a dozen books, most of them popular works dealing with renewal and other contemporary spiritual issues, with titles like *From Holy Laughter to Holy Fire: America on the Edge of Revival* and *Whatever Happened to the Power of God: Is the Charismatic Church Slain in the Spirit or Down for the Count?*

But he has also written dozens of scholarly articles for journals and reference works, including twenty-eight biographies of minor Talmudic rabbis for the *Oxford Dictionary of Jewish Religion* and entries on several Hebrew words for Zondervan's *New International Dictionary of Old Testament Theology and Exegesis.*

Equally comfortable whether he is preaching from the pulpit of a pentecostal church in South Korea or giving a lecture to students at Fuller Theological Seminary's School of World Mission, where he served as a visiting professor of Jewish Apologetics, Brown is happy straddling the usually unbridgeable chasm between academia and ecclesia, even if he does occasionally feel as if he's lost in space.

"God has called me to be in both worlds," says Brown, sitting in his big, book-lined School of Ministry office. "At times, I feel like a cross between a sumo wrestler and a ballet dancer. One day I'll be lecturing in a seminary, and the next I'll be preaching to masses of people, with thousands of them lying in front of the altar, and the sick being healed. I know I am called to run both races well."

And for Brown, much of his life does resemble a race. He has a busy travel schedule, puts in long hours at both the school and revival services, and spends the hours between eleven and four writing his articles and books. (That's the hours between 11 P.M. and 4 A.M., by the way, and he may start even later than that if revival meetings continue past midnight.)

"I can't rest until the world hears the gospel, Israel accepts Jesus, and the Lord comes back," he says.

During services at Brownsville Assembly, Brown serves as a walking, talking encyclopedia of Bible knowledge and revival lore, with both evangelist Steve Hill and pastor John Kilpatrick stopping themselves in mid-sentence to check an Old Testament reference or historical anecdote with their resident scholar.

They—along with Brown himself—are thankful that he failed in his attempt to kill himself during a bad mescaline trip when he was sixteen years old.

As he tells it in his self-published testimony, *From LSD to PhD*, it was early one morning during September 1971 when Brown—the son of a Conservative Jewish father who served as the senior lawyer in the New York Supreme Court—tried to end his life. His ravenous appetite for heroin and hallucinogens had earned him the nickname Drug Bear. But deep down inside, Brown felt he was falling into an abyss. "I thought I was losing my mind," he says.

After partying with friends one night, his system full of mind-altering substances, he was unable to find his way home. In desperation, he tried to end it all by flinging himself in front of a passing car. The car happened to be driven by his parents, who rescued their son. Brown believed that God had something better in mind. "Less than one year later, I was living for God and telling people about Jesus, the Messiah and Lord of both Gentile and Jew."

Asked if he has any thoughts about the fact that both he and revival evangelist Steve Hill turned to God after years of drug abuse, he replied: "That was the case for many people who came to Christ during the Jesus movement," says Brown. "And my experience is that some of the people who were radical in the world are just as radical for God after they get saved."

Brown's conversion did not go over too well with his Jewish parents. And his efforts to convert a Jewish rabbi to his newfound faith did not fare much better, as he writes in *They Thought for Themselves,* a 1996 collection of stories of Jewish converts to Christianity:

> I knew beyond any doubt that my experience was real, but how could I answer his questions? What could I say when he told me that the English translation I was using was wrong, and that, time and time again, the New Testament writers misinterpreted the Hebrew Scriptures? He could read the original text. I couldn't! . . . (His) faith seemed to be ancient and authentic. Was mine?

It was Brown's zeal to evangelize Jews that led him to academia and the study of ancient languages. By 1982 he already had a bachelor's and a master's degree and was starting work on his doctorate, when he realized he was becoming intellectually proud:

> I could correct anybody, but I was becoming increasingly theo-
> logically oriented at the expense of my spiritual life. The Bible
> was more of a theological work than a living Word. God began
> to show me that I had lost my passion, and that scholarship had
> become something of an idol rather than a tool.

Brown repented of his idolatry and began seeking God anew. Later that year, as he was preaching at a small charismatic church, "the Spirit fell and people were filled with the Spirit. I myself was transformed."

Brown has been both an active student and a participant in spiritual renewal activities ever since. In 1994 he founded his ICN Ministries, Inc. (which stands for Israel, the Church, and the Nations).

And it was his desire to be more than a mere observer of God's work in the world that led him to Brownsville in 1996. "Based on what I had heard about Brownsville, I was hopeful and optimistic about what I would find there," he says. "But I was also cautious about getting my hopes up. But I promised God that if I found it was for real, I was going to dive in. And here I am."

Today Brown remains a unique advocate for the importance of the life of the mind in a pentecostal subculture that has tra- ditionally placed more emphasis on matters of the heart.

"Pentecostals often underemphasize the academic side of things, while evangelicals usually overemphasize it," he says. "Sure, we could do better scholarship in our pentecostal churches, but we have the fundamentals down solidly."

Training Men and Women for Ministry

Brown says that God called him to raise up the Brownsville Revival School of Ministry and gave him a strategic vision:

We are to entrench: the revival must go deeper. We are to expand: we need more workers and larger facilities. We need to equip: preparing laborers for the harvest. And we need to export: sending out workers with revival fire to the ends of the earth.

The school opened with 120 students in January 1997, but by the fall of 1998, it had grown to more than one thousand students from forty-six states and half a dozen foreign countries. Although most of the students are in their late teens and early twenties, some are in their sixties and seventies, with many having left homes and careers to attend the school. Brown says as many as half of the students either came to a saving faith in Christ through the Brownsville revival or experienced an awakening of their faith there.

He also says the school has had to turn away some students who lacked sufficient grounding in the faith—or in reality:

> Here's who is eligible to attend the school. First, make sure you're saved. Next, make sure God is calling you. And finally, if you're a flake, repent first. And when you grow up, come back, and we'll pour our lives into you.

In many ways the students at the school are trying to find an appropriate balance between academic exploration and spiritual experience, just as Brown did himself.

Classes are held Tuesdays through Fridays. The school day begins at noon because all the students are involved in revival services, which can last until one in the morning, or later. Chapel, which begins the week, is supposed to last an hour, but if it goes overtime, classes are shortened accordingly.

Students at the school sign up for a two-year program leading to an Associate of Arts degree in Practical Ministry. At the end of their studies they will have completed most courses required for ordination in the Assemblies of God, if they choose to go that route.

Classes explore the Old and New Testaments, Christian doctrine, youth ministry, missions, cross-cultural communication, and leadership. In addition, Brown teaches classes on Christianity's Jewish roots and "Giants of the Faith." Larry Tomczak, who was a pioneer of the charismatic renewal movement of the 1960s and 1970s, lectures on the Christian family and divine healing. And David Ravenhill, son of the late Leonard Ravenhill, teaches on prayer and intercession.

The school also offers nonaccredited Distance Education Courses, enabling those who cannot commit to full-time studies to learn from audio- and videotapes. In addition, the school has summer sessions. In 1998 nearly two thousand students attended seven four-day sessions on topics like Revival and Reformation, Praise and Worship, Signs and Wonders, and Winning the Lost at Any Cost.

The emphasis on practical tools that can help people minister to others permeates the curriculum says John Cava, the school's director of missions. "We're trying to take the fruit of the revival and mold lives that have a passion to reach out to others. We want our students to really understand the outside world, not just have a unique revival experience here."

One way Cava helps students understand the outside world is by organizing missions trips and internships at dozens of domestic and foreign sites. During one 1998 chapel, two groups of students spoke about their recent ministry experiences.

First, three students talked about their fifteen-day stints as hospital chaplaincy interns at the Louisiana State University Medical Center in Shreveport. "We saw death, and we saw some gruesome stuff," said one student. "But when the Lord calls you to something, the Lord's gifts begin to flow." Chaplain Ann Montes, who supervised the students, said, "Without exception, those in the hospital were enriched by their precious ministry in our midst."

Next, more than a dozen students described their experiences on a recent school-organized missions trip to Mexico. Many said the trip to a nearby but radically different country forced them to come to grips with the way culture can influence people's belief and practice. "Before this, I never knew how much America we have in us that's not biblical," said one student, crying as she spoke. "I never knew. But the Lord used this trip to help me rediscover the Holy Spirit and to deepen my commitment to serving Him on the mission field."

During the School of Revival's 1998 summer break, more than three hundred students participated in overseas missions trips to places like Mexico, Malaysia, Peru, China, Russia, Brazil, Mongolia, Italy, Scotland, France, Japan, and Germany. Many of these trips lasted for a month or more.

The school's students probably would not be able to compete academically with graduates of more traditional seminaries, where there is much more emphasis on the study of biblical languages and hermeneutics, systematic theology, and non-revival-related church history. But Brown believes their two years of studies will equip them to fan out across the globe, spreading the fire of revival and renewal.

"We want to be as practical as we can," he says. "We're doing the best we can with what we've got, which is what God's doing with all of us."

Fire: Handle with Caution

Brown and the other instructors at the Brownsville Revival School of Ministry are trying to discipline and train their enthusiastic students without quenching their fervor. The readings and exercises the teachers assign are designed to channel and guide the students' passion for serving God and ministering to the world without snuffing it out altogether.

In doing so, these instructors are following in the footsteps of revival leaders from centuries past, many of whom saw education and spiritual awakening as allied forces for rejuvenating the church and transforming society.

In the 1730s William Tennent Sr., an Irish-born Scotsman who had emigrated to America in 1716, erected a log building on his Pennsylvania farm and began educating his three sons there, along with a dozen other young men. Skeptics—and there were many—ridiculed Tennent's efforts, mockingly calling his effort the "Log College." But Tennent's sons Gilbert, John, and William Jr. "graduated" from that simple school to become influential Presbyterian leaders and important figures in the Great Awakening.

As a result of that Awakening, many young men were converted, felt a call to the ministry, and went to college to study. In doing so, they increased enrollments at Yale, Harvard, and William and Mary—the earliest of the continent's colonial colleges—and helped stimulate the founding of other early colleges, including Princeton (founded by Presbyterians), Brown University (founded by Baptists as Rhode Island College), and Rutgers (founded as Queen's College by members of the Dutch Reformed Church).

Gilbert Tennent, who accompanied evangelist George Whitefield during the latter's 1740–41 preaching tour of the colonies, was one of many such young men to study at Yale. His most famous (and perhaps most controversial) sermon, "The Danger of an Unconverted Ministry," stressed the importance of both the academic and the spiritual aspects of education:

Such who are contented under a dead Ministry, have not in them the Temper of that Saviour they profess. It's an awful Sign, that they are as blind as Moles, and as dead as Stones, without any spiritual Taste and Relish . . .

And let those who live under the Ministry of dead Men, whether they have got the Form of Religion or not, repair to the Living, where they may be edified.

During America's Second Great Awakening, Timothy Dwight—a grandson of Jonathan Edwards—illustrated the important links between revival and education. Dwight served as president of Yale from 1795 until his death in 1817. Shortly after he came to Yale, students at the school experienced a series of awakenings. In part the revivals were spurred by Dwight's powerful, emotional preaching (a genetic inheritance, perhaps?). Specifically, Dwight railed against philosophical skepticism and the denial that God had inspired the text of the Bible.

During the 1830s Charles Finney stressed the importance of educating people for the ministry in his lectures on revival. In his lecture on "Hindrances to Revival," Finney described a number of factors that could cause a revival to end.

When a Church rejects the calls of God upon it for educating young men for the ministry, it will hinder and destroy a revival . . . God pours His Spirit on the Churches, and converts hundreds of thousands of souls, and if then the labourers do not come forth into the harvest, what can be expected but that the curse of God will come upon the churches, and His Spirit will be withdrawn, and revivals will cease?

During the nineteenth and twentieth centuries, Christian renewal movements and evangelistic crusades led by leaders like Dwight Moody and Charles Fuller resulted in the creation of dozens of new schools, Bible colleges, conferences, and networks of believers.

Staying on Fire for God

Brown continually returns to two themes, regardless of whether he is giving a mini-sermon to thousands at one of Brownsville's revival services, delivering an inspirational talk to hundreds of students during a Brownsville Revival School of Ministry chapel service, or lecturing a dozen divinity students in a small classroom at an evangelical seminary.

One is that the passionate flame of devotion to God need not die out or fade away. "God's call is for us to remain hot and fervent," he says.

Another is that the purpose of God's infilling and empowering is not for our own selfish enjoyment, but rather for the redemption of the world. "The Brownsville experience is not so you have a story to tell people ten years from now. This is so you can be spiritually launched into orbit."

In a talk entitled "How to Stay on Fire for God," Brown discusses chapter 12 of Paul's letter to the Romans ("present your bodies a living sacrifice, holy, acceptable to God . . . [and be] fervent in spirit," vv. 1, 11) and emphasizes the following practical points.

Put God First

"Developing and maintaining your relationship with God must be the first priority in your life," he says. While Brown says relating to God must be more important than your career or your family, that does not mean everyone should flee all earthly responsibilities. "It's not just about time, but it's about the attitude of your heart and the priority of your life. Your relationship with God should be the thing around which everything else in your life is built."

Part of putting God first means dealing thoroughly with those things that stand in the way, and in America, one of the main challenges to loving God is the frenzied pace of our lives. "You must cultivate quality times with God as well as quantity times," he says.

In addition, Brown advocates fasting—both from food and from the mass media. "The news published in newspapers happened whether you read it or not," he says, supporting his thought with an anecdote Tozer used to tell about Thoreau. "Someone once asked Thoreau if he would like a newspaper. He replied, 'No, I've already seen one.'"

Brown says he is not advocating that believers be culturally illiterate. "We're in this world, and we're not just supposed to walk through it like zombies." But as with most pentecostal leaders of the twentieth century, he believes that missing out on today's news, entertainment, or sports is less of a crime than missing out on quality time alone with God.

Be Sensitive to Sin

"Be quick to recognize symptoms of backsliding," he says, pointing out that most fires do not die out immediately, but cool down gradually:

> A consistent lack of discipline will lead to a serious fall. Don't be like the guy who says, "Gosh, I can't figure out why I just murdered my neighbor!" Don't allow yourself to gradually become a little more accustomed to sin.
>
> Instead, at the first sign of sin creeping in, be ruthless and don't make excuses. Be quick to repent. Be quick to obey the Spirit's prompting. You don't want to become hard. And you don't want to become like the man who is driving his car, misses his turn, but keeps driving the wrong direction for another three hours anyway. Once you realize you're going the wrong way, be quick to repent. Be quick to turn around.

Stay Near the Fire (but Without Being Foolish)

Brown does not claim to understand all the ways of God, but

he does believe that—for whatever reasons—God periodically chooses to bless certain churches and ministries in powerful ways. Today that blessing might fall at Brownsville; tomorrow it might fall someplace else. That's fine with him.

"We don't think Brownsville is the only thing happening, but something unique is happening here. We see what's happening at Brownsville as part of a larger complex of revival and renewal that God is involved in around the world."

Brown believes it is essential for believers to stay near a vibrant, Spirit-filled congregation if they want to remain passionate for God themselves. "Everything produces fruit after its own kind," he says. "And you need to get yourself somewhere or get into something where the Spirit is moving."

On the other hand, Brown has a powerful disdain for unstable believers who flit from one "revival" to another in an endless search for something special from God. He calls such people "Holy Spirit zap addicts," and he wishes they would grow up.

"They're like drug addicts sitting around talking about their latest high," says Brown, who used to engage in such discussions himself. "You don't have to go around the world to be touched by God."

Next, he launches into a tirade against these spiritual thrill seekers:

> You say you're talking or praying in tongues, but you may be sitting there thinking about an error in the checkbook, or a show featuring the Three Stooges. You were just going through the motions. You were just mumbling . . .
>
> It would be great if every time you pray, the building shakes, the roof opens, and a dove comes down. But if you tell me that happens to you everyday, I'll tell you you're weird.

Move Onward and Upward

"Keep setting your standards higher," says Brown. "Always

have an attitude of 'Forward march!' Keep hungering and thirsting for more of God."

Brown says one way people can keep on moving on is by studying the lives of some of the great missionaries and revivalists Brown teaches about in his "Giants of the Faith" course. "Their examples challenge me to go deeper, and their lives will challenge you to go further."

Serve God and Humanity

God does not want a bunch of "zap addicts," says Brown. Instead, He wants loyal and devoted servants. "Give away what you have. Find ways to lose your life and let God's power flow out of you. Don't be a selfish grumbler and complainer."

Step Out with God

"Learn to enjoy the adventure of faith," he says, citing the example of a tentative Peter walking on the water with his Lord. "I'm not talking about foolishness, like not taking the medicine your doctor has prescribed and seeing if you will die.

"What I'm talking about is developing a lifestyle that is always getting ready to get out of the boat and go walking on the water with Jesus. And remember: God promises to finish what He started."

Many students find Brown's ideas about ongoing renewal and empowerment moving. In addition, they find inspiration in his personal commitment to live the high standards he teaches. But sometimes people misunderstand him, mistaking his zealous earnestness for a theology of works. But Brown believes any spirituality that can be worked up with human willpower is doomed to fail. Humans are fallible, he reminds them. Only God's love is reliable.

"This is not legalism," he says. "God doesn't have us on some kind of tightrope. Instead, He wants us to live in the ocean of His grace and mercy."

And like his students, Brown is not standing on the beach waiting for the ocean's waves to come to him. He is jumping and splashing around in the water like a fish, and inviting others to hurry up and jump in with him.

And it's not just people at Brownsville who are being impacted by the revival there. Increasingly, its effects are spreading, as we will see in the next section.

Changed Lives

God got a hold of her

Like hundreds of others, Brooke Lash got saved at the revival and now attends Brownsville Revival School of Ministry.

The Best Years of Their Lives

Brooke Lash had thought her senior year in high school would be the best year of her life. The pretty and popular homecoming attendant had plenty of friends of both sexes, and plenty to do.

"But my senior year was my worst year of high school," she

says. "I really felt lonely. I was sick all the time. I didn't feel good. And I started to drink and party a little bit more."

At the time she didn't know it, but now, looking back, Brooke says, "It was God trying to get hold of me." With a grandfather who was a preacher and an aunt who was a youth pastor, Brooke knew plenty about Christianity.

"I knew God was for real, and I knew the things I was doing were wrong," she says. "But I thought when I got older it would be easier to make things right. In the meantime, I avoided every question about it. I thought I was having too much fun, but God showed me I wasn't."

Brooke had heard about the revival in Pensacola, and when Brownsville pastor John Kilpatrick came to speak in her home-town of Mobile, Alabama, in May 1996, she went to hear what he had to say. "God really started working in my heart that night," she says. "I went down to the altar, but I don't think I made a real commitment."

That came about a week later. In May she and a group of fifteen kids went to one of Brownsville's Thursday evening youth services. "I knew what I was going there to do. When they gave the call, I ran down the steps and went to the altar. I knew there was no chance to turn back now. There were no other choices for me."

The next month Brooke persuaded her two best friends, Marissa and Sandi, to go to revival services at Brownsville with her. "It was hard," she says. "I had to pay for a hotel room for a weekend and tell them we could also go to the beach. But they decided to come."

Both girls went forward to get right with God. And in January 1997, all three girls signed up for the first semester of classes at the Brownsville Revival School of Ministry.

There, Brooke and her two closest friends now experience the deep joy they never knew during their senior year. Brooke, in fact, is one of the most fervent and energetic worshipers in a school full of a thousand people who are ga-ga for God. "I'm just praising Him," she says of her enthusiastic dancing and jumping. "He created us to worship Him. He created my feet. He created my legs. He created my arms. He created my hands. He created my mouth—all for Him."

In early 1998 Brooke was part of a school missions trip to Mexico. The trip touched her heart in strange and powerful ways, and confirmed her desire to serve God with her life. "I feel like God's calling me to be a missionary," she says, "but I don't know where."

PART III

Assessing Brownsville's Impact and Legacy

*Revival has spread from Brownsville to churches throughout America
and around the world.*

CHAPTER NINE

The Ripple Effect:

The Spreading Impact of the Brownsville Revival

A single drop of water falling on the surface of a calm pond can create dozens of concentric circles, rippling outward to the water's banks. A sudden downpour, however, can create thousands of overlapping undulations, and can even raise the level of the entire pond, causing it to overflow its banks and inundate the surrounding land.

Likewise, revival can be described as a sudden and dramatic spiritual deluge, flooding in on a group or a congregation, raising their levels of spiritual empowerment, and using them to shower others with spiritual blessings.

Those periods in church history that we now regard as revivals were more than short-term, localized outbursts. Instead, they were extended seasons of spiritual drenching, which had a profound impact on individuals, churches, and the larger society.

Today there is no doubt among historians that America's Great Awakenings were movements that had that kind of broad-based impact. Likewise, the Azusa Street revival of the early 1900s spawned a worldwide movement, earning it a secure spot in the history books.

The jury is still out, however, on more recent movements such as the Jesus movement and charismatic movement of the 1960s and 1970s. Those who were personally impacted by one or both of these will certainly declare them to be profoundly important, but historians still wait and watch. And it is way too soon to tell about the Brownsville revival, a movement that is still going strong—at least it was in 1998 as these words were written. But a preliminary look at the revival and its effects thus far makes it at least a strong candidate for inclusion in the revival hall of fame.

Indeed, since it began in June 1995, the Brownsville revival has spread its spiritual impact far beyond the Pensacola area and the southeastern United States. Increasingly, people and churches from throughout the country and the world claim to have been transformed by it. In a very real sense, the ripples of revival have spread out from Brownsville until some of them have spread over the rest of the globe.

One of the clearest indications that something interesting is going on in Pensacola is the extensive media coverage the revival has received. Newspapers, magazines, and TV shows have done hundreds of stories about what is happening at Brownsville. Initially, the stories described a religious awakening that was newsworthy largely because it was novel. But more recent media coverage has portrayed the revival as an event of truly historic proportions.

"Revivals come and go, but what has been happening here, night after night . . . is different," wrote Rick Bragg in his May 1997 page-one piece in *The New York Times* entitled, "In Florida, a Revival That Came but Didn't Go." Bragg said, "What started as a typical, temporary revival on Father's Day 1995 has snowballed into what is apparently the largest and longest-running pentecostal revival in America in almost a century."

USA Today writer Deborah Sharp, in her June 1997 article, "Fire and brimstone and the hand of God," also noted the revival's longevity, adding that its impact was spreading far and wide:

Members of every denomination imaginable have streamed to Pensacola in the past two years to be saved from damnation: Catholics, Methodists, Baptists and Buddhists. American Indians kneel beside Amish people, South Africans next to Koreans.

Charisma was the first national religious magazine to cover the revival, and was joined soon after by many others. Likewise, the revival and its repercussions have received prominent treatment in the *Pentecostal Evangel*, the weekly magazine published by the Assemblies of God, a denomination that has been transformed by the revival. And it's not just Assemblies churches that have been impacted. The Pensacola revival was the subject of a 1996 cover story in *Good News*, a magazine promoting spiritual renewal in American Methodism.

Ultimately, the only truly reliable measure of the validity and impact of the Brownsville revival is the test of time. Unfortunately, these results won't be in for decades. But those who want to make a tentative investigation of the Brownsville revival's fruits thus far can examine some of the preliminary results discussed later in this chapter.

But first, a review of earlier revivals and their effects will help us know what to look for.

Fruit of the Faith

Today, supporters of the idea that America is a Christian nation look back with affection at the pre-Revolutionary era that Jonathan Edwards called home. But to Edwards, who was both an observer and participant in the Great Awakening, times were tough and the nation's spiritual climate seemed to be getting worse by the day.

Little more than a century after English Puritans sailed to the New World to create "a city on a hill," things were not working out the way some had hoped. The bonds between church and state were rapidly unraveling only to be replaced by a novel and intoxicating combination of individualism and pluralism. There is no denying that the colonists of Edwards's day were a religious bunch, but as he and others saw it, public morals were in a nose-dive.

In his home town of Northampton, Massachusetts, the clear-est indicator of the town's declining spiritual state could be found among the colonies' youth, who were given to licentious-ness, night-walking, tavern-hopping, and a host of lewd prac-tices. In the 1730s, thanks in part to Edwards's own preaching, things began to turn around. Parents increasingly disciplined their young, and the children received this correction.

In 1738, when young George Whitefield made the first of his seven preaching tours of the colonies, small, localized awaken-ings like that in Northampton began to be linked to others else-where, resulting in a nationwide revival, which brought increased conversions, growing congregations, and an improved spiritual climate.

The moral improvements brought about by the Great Awaken-ing were neither universal nor permanent, but that does not mean they were not important. Historian Harry Stout refers to the Great Awakening as "the most momentous occasion in the spiritual life of colonial America." In addition, Stout and others argue that the Awakening also imbued the colonists with brave new democratic ideas about both public discourse and social authority—ideas that would become increasingly important as the colonies moved toward nationhood.

As the 1800s dawned, the young American nation faced a host of new challenges. Deism and skepticism were becoming increasingly popular in the cultured East, and for those brave souls who lived in the rough and rugged frontier West, there were lawlessness and lasciviousness on a scale that Edwards would have found shocking.

The Second Great Awakening, which lasted into the 1820s,

was orderly in the East but wild in the West, where camp meetings drew thousands to events featuring direct preaching and dramatic manifestations. In addition to launching new denominations, such as the Disciples of Christ, the revival inspired believers to create new ministries devoted to domestic and foreign missions efforts. Their work would change the face of the church in America and around the world. What's more, Christians influenced by the revivals were among those leading various social reform movements, such as the efforts to abolish slavery and improve the conditions of child workers.

At the beginning of the twentieth century, urbanization, industrialization, and secularism were giving the church new challenges. It was in Los Angeles, a city now synonymous with secularism at its gaudy worst, that the century's most important revival would take off.

There was nothing out of the ordinary about the handful of believers who gathered in the rundown warehouse on Azusa Street, but the extraordinary outpouring of spiritual gifts that were made manifest there launched the worldwide pentecostal movement, now one of the most potent forms of Christianity in the world. The Azusa Street revival launched some three hundred new denominations, the largest of which is the Assemblies of God, now with more than fifteen million members worldwide.

Throughout history revival has inspired a dramatic deepening of individual spirituality, but it has also resulted in the founding of schools and colleges, increased financial giving and service to evangelistic and missions organizations, and often a deeper commitment to transforming the world, whether that meant serving meals to the destitute in a soup kitchen or working to free slaves from their bondage.

Compared to the renowned revival movements of the past, the Brownsville awakening is a scruffy newcomer barely out of training wheels. It is still too early to assess its impact. There is evidence, though, to suggest that it, too, may be gaining the kind of prominence and influence that might ultimately make it one for the history books.

Southern-Fried Sanctification

Pensacola is so far to the western end of the long Florida panhandle that it's less than a half hour away from Alabama. Drive another hour and you're in Mississippi. In these states—and in the entire surrounding region—sin and sanctification are not just terms theologians kick around; they're part of the common vernacular. And it's in this region that the Brownsville revival has probably had its greatest impact.

Most of the newspapers in the region have covered the revival, and many of the towns and cities within a two-hundred-mile radius are home to individuals who hopped in their cars, drove down to Brownsville, and met God there.

And while Pensacola's nearness to hundreds of miles of Gulf Coast beaches have long made it a popular jumping-off point for travelers and tourists, the revival has had a significant impact on the city's tourism industry. In 1997 the *Pensacola News Journal* reported that twelve thousand of the ninety-four thousand people visiting the Pensacola Beach Visitor's Center during one five-month period said they came to town to attend revival services. The paper also reported that when the revival went on a one-week hiatus, tourism officials saw a noticeable downturn in visitors.

Linda Fussel, a member of the Brownsville congregation, works for Global Travel, a Pensacola travel agency that has had to add an agent to handle revival-related calls. Fussell says the agency handles as many as a hundred calls a day from people calling to make arrangements to visit the revival. The revival attracts many repeat visitors, including some who bring additional friends and family members along with them for their return visits.

Local hotels and restaurants offer Brownsville discounts. Steve Hill says car rental chains have received so many inquiries about directions to the church, they have revised the maps they hand out to their customers. And chartered buses are a regular sight in the church parking lots.

And far away from Brownsville in cities like Houston, Denver, Anaheim, and Toledo, revival leaders have been presenting Awake America rallies, which are designed to spread the revival's effects throughout the land. Each of the rallies, which began in 1997, has attracted thousands of faithful and curious, although it's impossible to tell if they have had any deeper impact.

Over the years, revival leaders have crowed about the effect the event has had on the Pensacola area, at times making claims that the revival has brought about a decrease in local crime, juvenile delinquency, and drug abuse. But city crime statistics do not support such claims, and even if there were significant declines in criminal activity, it would be another thing to conclusively correlate these changes to the revival alone. The neighborhood surrounding the church is still just about as run-down as it was before revival started. Down the street from the Brownsville church, an adult strip club thrives. And some of the neighbors who live near the church say the only difference the revival has made in their lives is that people park their cars on their yards and try to convert them to Christianity. "They're OK, but it gets kind of annoying," said one local.

There is no doubt that criminals, drug abusers, and prostitutes have attended the revival and had their lives transformed as a result. However, claims that the Brownsville revival has transformed its city seem to be either wishful thinking or an evangelistic boast.

A Denomination Reborn

The Assemblies of God is the biggest of the hundreds of pentecostal denominations to spring from the Azusa Street revival, and has more than 2.5 million members in America and another 12.5 million members worldwide.

Originally, many of the people who experienced a deeper spiritual life as a result of the Azusa Street revival sought to stay in their existing churches and denominations and renew them. But contention over the gifts of the Holy Spirit made such efforts impossible. In 1914 approximately three hundred individuals gathered at a convention in Hot Springs, Arkansas, where they created the General Council of the Assemblies of God.

It was rapid worldwide growth from then on. During the 1940s, the denomination joined the National Association of Evangelicals, symbolizing its desire to be a part of the Christian mainstream rather than a solitary movement. Throughout much of the 1970s, the denomination was one of the fastest growing in the world.

In the 1980s, however, troubles hit hard. Jim Bakker and Jimmy Swaggart, two Assemblies-ordained ministers, built huge religious broadcasting empires only to suffer humiliating public setbacks involving sex and money. When Bakker and Swaggart refused to submit to the denomination's authority and follow its discipline, both men were defrocked. At the same time, decades of constant growth began to level out.

"The Assemblies of God was raised up as a revival movement, but we had moved away from that," says General Superintendent Thomas Trask, the denomination's highest-ranking official. "We had become content. We had become careless. We had cooled off." During the late 1980s and early 1990s, the denomination's growth stopped. Trask and others grew concerned. "We had plateaued, and there was some indication that things were beginning to go the other way."

The revival at Brownsville came just in time. Hundreds of Assemblies pastors have visited the revival, experienced a dramatic touch of God there, and returned to their churches refreshed and spiritually renewed. "This is really a sovereign move of God, and the impact has been powerful," says Trask. "Many, many of our pastors have gone searching, looking, and believing, and they have witnessed the power of God. It has done something for their own hearts and lives."

It has also done something for church statistics. In 1996 and 1997 the denomination reported significant increases in conversions, water baptisms, and Spirit baptisms. And giving for foreign missions is at an all-time high: 117 million dollars.

Another consequence of the revival is that churches in the Assemblies of God have begun receiving criticism for the enthusiasm of their worship and the fervor of their members—charges that have not been leveled against many Assemblies congregations for decades. And Trask loves it.

"I'd rather deal with these kinds of excesses than with death," he says. "Life is much easier to deal with than death. I'll take the revival any day and deal with the challenges that come with that."

But not all in the Assemblies agree. Hundreds of pastors who have streamed to Brownsville in search of personal spiritual renewal have returned to their home churches hoping to duplicate the spiritual power they experienced in Pensacola. While that has worked in many cases, in others it has caused pain and division.

A member of one Assembly of God church told me that her pastor's effort to reproduce Brownsville "has wreaked spiritual havoc in our church." In this case, members who were not sure what to make of the changes were charged with "quenching the Spirit" by a "spiritually correct" group that assumed greater leadership powers and gradually removed from ministry those who did not toe the revival line. "The fervor to force-feed a congregation can be difficult to believe until you've experienced it firsthand." But still, after more than a year of effort, revival has not caught hold. "The church, which had been steadily growing, has stagnated. Almost half of the members have left. And finally, our pastor resigned to take another church. Now we are left with a divided, wounded flock in search of a shepherd."

In spite of such episodes, most in the denomination seem to support the Brownsville revival and the renewal in many of the Assemblies' churches. Revival has been a major story in the denominational magazine, the *Pentecostal Evangel*, America's largest weekly religious periodical with a circulation of 250,000. The magazine now provides regular "revival updates," and reports have included coverage of Assemblies congregations in Iowa, Illinois, Montana, Oklahoma, Kentucky, Texas, California, Michigan, Virginia, Arizona, Pennsylvania, New York, Indiana, Washington, Georgia, and elsewhere.

Joel Kilpatrick (who is no relation to Brownsville pastor John Kilpatrick) joined the staff of the *Pentecostal Evangel* in 1996, a time when the Brownsville revival was starting to take off and the magazine was busy reporting on the impact it was having throughout the denomination. "Calls started coming in from pastors all over the country who had gone to Brownsville," says Kilpatrick. "They would tell me, 'I didn't do anything but get up behind the pulpit and start speaking, and all of a sudden, the Spirit came down on us and brought revival to our church too.'"

In the process of covering revival, Kilpatrick himself has been revived. One pastor calls him "someone who was reporting on the river and fell in." As Kilpatrick tells it, the revival could not have come at a better time for his denomination, or his own spiritual journey.

The grandson of a pentecostal pastor, and the son of a man who is ordained by the Assemblies of God, Kilpatrick had grown up hearing stories of the denomination's past spiritual glories, which were a stark contrast to the reality of contemporary church life. "I sometimes felt like the people around me were following the momentum from an old spiritual impetus I had never experienced," he says.

But Kilpatrick began to see hints of the historic fervor at Assemblies congregations in New York and California. Assigned to write stories about churches experiencing revival, he began to develop an increasing desire to be renewed himself. "I began setting aside an hour on Saturday evenings to be still and wait for the Lord," he says. Kilpatrick and his wife also began personally recognizing the Holy Spirit in their prayers, asking Him to lead their lives.

During a prayer time with denominational leaders who had come to Springfield in 1997 from around the nation, Kilpatrick experienced a breakthrough. "For the first time in my life, I felt like God was beneath the ceiling," he says. "Before, my prayers had always seemed to bounce off the ceiling. But now, God's presence was here." That experience was followed by many more in which Kilpatrick felt the closeness of the Lord. Gradually, the God of his fathers was becoming a powerful reality in his own life.

"For the first time I knew that the Lord was real and that He loved me," he says. "Now my life has radically changed. I never dreamed life could have as much meaning to me as it does now. The Lord is more real to me than most people are. I love Him.

"There was a long period where I questioned the church. Now I see there was a wisdom here I had not been able to see, but the Lord revealed it to me."

The Flame Spreads

It's not just congregations in the Assemblies of God that have been impacted by the revival at Brownsville. As one Assemblies theology professor wrote: "When [revival] happens, the effects

are never confined to a single congregation or denomination—
nor does God intend them to be. Revival is not the exclusive
property of one part of the church."

Many thousands of people from dozens of denominations
have attended Awake America rallies sponsored by and featuring Brownsville revival leaders John Kilpatrick, Steve Hill,
Lindell Cooley, and Michael Brown. The rallies, which represent the leaders' efforts to respond to the many speaking invitations they receive, were held in nearly a dozen cities in 1997 and
1998.

In addition, thousands of pastors from hundreds of denominations and dozens of countries have attended Brownsville
revival services, or one of the church's pastor conferences, which
are held about twice a year. During one 1996 Sunday morning
service at the church, Pastor Kilpatrick asked people to share
their testimonies. A man who identified himself as a pastor from
England stood up and told his story:

> A few years ago, I had the fire. But somewhere along the way it
> left. People make demands on you. They just drain you. After a
> while you're just going through the motions. But now, I know that
> God's unfolding a lovely plan for my life. I just want to go back
> and live for Jesus.

This pastor's story—with both its paralyzing fatigue and its
energizing renewal—could be repeated many times over. And an
article in the March 1998 issue of *Charisma* magazine gave anec-
dotal accounts of three British pastors who visited Brownsville.
Gary Black, who pastors Callender Christian Fellowship in
Scotland, told the magazine, "God really surprised me by revealing something of what He intends for my ministry."

Not all the pastors who have been to Brownsville have traveled around the globe. For Perry Dalton and Linda Smith of the

Pine Forest United Methodist Church, visiting Brownsville merely required a crosstown jaunt.

Dalton, the senior pastor of the church, was out of town when the revival hit, but youth pastor Linda Smith began attending with members of her youth group early on. The impact was immediate. Smith found her spiritual life deepened, and her kids were profoundly touched too. Dalton, who originally visited Brownsville just to see what Smith was talking about, found himself moved as well. Dalton and Smith decided they needed to be as involved as they could, and a mutually supportive relationship developed between the two churches.

"There is a real ecumenical spirit between Brownsville and our church," said Dalton. "There was no effort to steal sheep away." Now Dalton and other local pastors try to help out at Brownsville, some volunteering to assist at the prayer services that can last for hours after Steve Hill's sermons, and others assisting at Friday evening baptismal services.

One would not necessarily know it today, but Methodism has strong historical links to the kind of revivalism seen at Brownsville. Founders John and Charles Wesley were introduced to a deeper relationship with Christ through their friendship with some Moravian believers. Transformed by their experiences and committed to finding "methods" for spreading renewal to others, the Wesleys traveled and preached throughout their native England, founding numerous Methodist societies and teaching others to promote their teachings on Christian holiness and follow their practical procedures.

Francis Asbury, the first Methodist general superintendent in America, was even more of a tireless traveler than the Wesleys. Crisscrossing the rugged American countryside to preach to the unconverted and help establish Methodist societies, Asbury was an ardent supporter of camp meetings, which he believed were an effective vehicle for communicating the gospel and convicting people of sin.

With his religious fervor and his passion for saving the lost, Asbury played a central role in American Methodism's growth and spread throughout the continent. Today, however, many Methodists would hardly recognize the faith of their fathers. Many observers believe this historic and theological amnesia has been a major factor in the church's decades-long membership declines, as well as its divisive debates over issues like homosexuality.

Growing from Someone Else's Revival

Steve Beard is the editor of *Good News*, the magazine published by the Good News organization, a renewal group trying to help United Methodists remember their heritage.

Beard has a solid grasp of his denomination's evangelical roots, and he attempted to spell out some of the connections between historic Methodism and contemporary revivals in his 1997 book, *Thunderstruck: John Wesley and the Pensacola Outpouring*.

Although designed for readers from Wesleyan backgrounds, the book offers practical advice to any and all about approaching and appreciating revivals, no matter the denomination in which they occur. Among Beard's tips are the following.

Be Supportive of Movements of the Spirit

Just as Asbury supported camp meetings, the Wesleys supported open-air preaching—even though it was controversial at the time—because it helped people hear the gospel who would not otherwise hear it. If the kingdom of God is being extended, do not worry so much about all the particulars of how God does that.

Go Beyond Your Own Group

Many Christians do not have very much contact with believers from other churches or theological traditions, but the Wesleys were interested in what God was doing, no matter where it was happening. Perhaps more of us could express greater interest in and sensitivity to the things God is doing outside the walls of our own church.

Allow God to Work

Human rituals and traditions can be beautiful reminders of God's work with believers throughout history, but they can also be barriers to His involvement in our churches and our lives today. By temperament, John Wesley was rigid and detail-oriented, but his passion to see people know God overpowered his own predilections. "I trust we shall all suffer God to carry on His work in the way that pleaseth Him," wrote Wesley.

Don't Grieve the Spirit

Wesley frequently asked God to forgive him for judging the spiritual behavior of others too quickly and too harshly. Don't repeat his error yourself. But if you do fall into judgment of what God is doing with others, be as quick as Wesley was to repent and ask God for forgiveness.

Test the Spirits

On the other hand, not all spirits are of God, and not all human religious behavior is divinely inspired. Wesley was not fooled by unusual manifestations, but tested everything against the testimony of God in Scripture and the evidence of the spiritual fruit found in people's lives.

Spread the Good News of God's Amazing Acts

If you see God transform someone's life, let someone else know about it. Broadcasting accounts of God's awakening power may cause others to seek Him and ultimately experience that power themselves.

But what happens when revival looks like bad news instead of a divine awakening? We will explore some of revivalism's excesses next.

Changed Lives

The fire strikes Missouri

Pastors Steve and Kathy Gray were burned out and frustrated before Steve's visit to Brownsville brought encouragement to them and renewal to their congregation.

Raising the Dead

Some nights, hundreds of pastors attend revival services at Brownsville Assembly of God. Most of them sit together in a big section of specially reserved pews. But when pastor Steve Gray first walked into the sanctuary in March 1996, he did not want anybody to know he was a pastor.

"I came here the most miserable man on the face of the earth," he says. "I thought, *God is finished with me. And if He's not finished with me, I'm finished with me.* I was a deeply wounded, deeply discouraged man."

As Steve saw it, he had plenty to be upset about. His marriage to Kathy had been through its share of ups and downs, and was currently under stress. And his own spiritual life was bone dry. Yet the main reason for Steve's despair was the situation back at Smithton Community Church in Smithton, a tiny town in central Missouri.

Built in 1859, the church had been vacant for years until 1984, when Steve turned down a lucrative offer from a Chicago church and accepted Smithton's invitation to become the church's pastor, a move he believed was an act of obedience to God.

He remembers praying about the choice on the floor of his home. "Lord, here's Chicago. Big church. Nice house. Good money. And over here is Smithton. No people. No money. Nothing. What would You do?" Steve recalls God's answer as if it came yesterday: "I'll tell you what I would do. I would raise the dead."

By 1996 the church was not dead. In fact, on the surface everything looked great. Attendance was strong. Financial giving was solid. Praise and worship were lively.

But Steve and Kathy were struggling. A congregational tiff Kathy calls "a hurtful incident" led a handful of members to leave the church. Other members did not seem to even notice the episode, but it left Steve crushed and hopeless. Meanwhile, revival—something Steve had been praying for for more than a decade—had never come.

Steve went to Pensacola and stayed there for ten days, praying in his hotel room by day and attending revival services at night. Two nights in a row, Steve says he heard God speak to him, saying, "I want you to have a revival." Steve did not understand, since he was at a spiritual low point in his life. Then, on the third night, God gave further clarification: "I didn't say I want you to *be* a revival. I said I want you to *have* a revival." Steve felt comforted that he merely had to host a revival, not drum one up by his own effort.

Unsure what was going to happen next, Steve returned to Smithton. It was 6:12 P.M. on March 24, 1996, when Steve entered his church. The Sunday evening service had just started. As he walked toward Kathy, something happened. "Before I could even touch her, the fire of God struck me like lightning from heaven." Next, Steve began to jump up and down, with every hurt and discouragement falling off him like so many scales. Then, the energy that manifested itself when he approached his wife started to reach other members of the congregation.

No one was sure what to make of all this, so they came back the next night to pray about it, and the next night, and the next. They've been coming back five nights a week ever since, and joining them have been thousands of visitors from across America and around the world.

"We have more people in our building than we do in our town," says Gray, who has been featured in magazines like *Charisma* and *Christianity Today*.

And it's not just members and visitors who are being touched by God. The Grays are being blessed as well. "It's true revival when the pastor's wife gets revival," says Kathy.

During the Grays' 1998 visit to Brownsville, pastor John Kilpatrick asked Steve and Kathy to come up to the church's pulpit and share their story. They did, ending their comments with expressions of gratefulness to the church and to God.

"Thank you to the vessels here," said Steve, "and to the Lord. Thank you!"

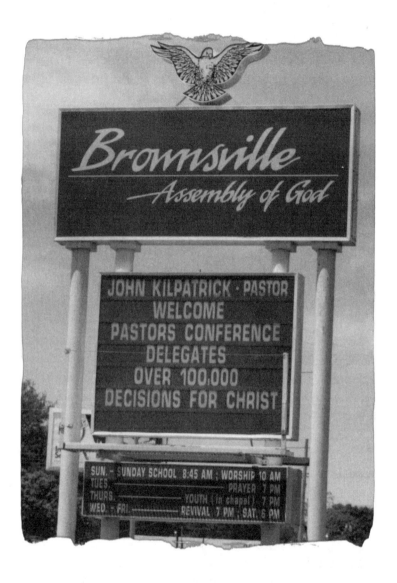

The sign out in front of the church doesn't match McDonald's claim of "billions served," but it has tried to keep track of decisions. The numbers shown here were posted when the revival was one year old.

CHAPTER TEN

Ghosts of Elmer Gantry:

Exploring Revivalism's Ugly Excesses

Revival is an important part of the history of Christianity, and today many believers regard major historic revivals with a mixture of reverence and pride. But revivalism also has a dark side, and the conspicuous misdeeds of those who claim to speak for God has been a constant source of shame and embarrassment to faithful followers of Christ.

When a preacher falls—whether a high-tech televangelist or an old-fashioned tent revivalist—that's news, even though it is a story that's nearly as old as the faith itself. And such real-life reversals provide Hollywood movie makers with plenty of raw material to draw from in creating sensationalistic depictions of the wretched side of the religion business.

Most of these movies feature one or all of the following: showbizzy preachers whose lives stand in stark contrast to the message of righteousness they so powerfully preach; manipulative services and altar calls that ruthlessly exploit people's fears about the meaning of life and the mysteries of death but produce no lasting changes in their lives; high-pressure, lucrative offerings, which often appear to be designed to fund lavish lifestyles rather than the further spread of the gospel; and the ever-present fragrance of sexual immorality, which seems to cling to some evangelists like the stench of cheap cologne.

In 1997 actor Robert Duvall made film history with his critically acclaimed film, *The Apostle,* which was the first major American film to lavish the same kind of respectful attention on a Bible-thumping evangelist that Hollywood usually gives to stiletto-wielding serial killers and gun-toting gangsters. Duvall researched, wrote, directed, financed, and starred in the film about a southern pentecostal evangelist, Euliss "Sonny" Dewey—a sincere man who preaches the Word, dances in the Spirit, and saves white, black, and brown souls with a consuming zeal. "It's something I had to do," Duvall told me in a 1997 phone interview from his Virginia home. "We make great gangster movies, so why not make this kind of movie right too?"

Duvall's Euliss Dewey was not a saint. Instead he was a deeply flawed character who regularly cheated on his wife and engaged in other ministerial misdeeds.

Perhaps Duvall based part of his film's character on news accounts from the 1980s, when shocking revelations about the sad exploits of Jim Bakker and Jimmy Swaggart, two once-prominent Assemblies of God televangelists, were daily bread for both morning newspapers and late-night talk shows. As the stories multiplied, a picture emerged of religious hucksterism on a scale that would have baffled even the most cynical Hollywood scriptwriters. There were oversized egos, trysts with prostitutes and secretaries, large-dollar payoffs to secure silence and secrecy, air-conditioned doghouses and Imelda Marcos-size shoe collections, a casual disregard for both biblical ethics and the laws of the land, as well as a devilish disdain for the good-hearted people who consumed and supported it all.

With real-life men of God being seduced by the unholy trinity of money, sex, and power in such sensational ways, who needs movies?

During the past three and one-half years, the leaders of the Brownsville revival have come in for their share of criticism. None of them—at least so far—have been accused of sexual impropriety. But there have been serious questions, many of them raised by Pensacola's hometown newspaper, about how they have handled the millions of dollars that have flowed into revival-related businesses as spiritually hungry revival-goers have purchased books, videos, audiotapes, CDs, songbooks, manuals, and other products created in the wake of revival.

In November 1997 the *Pensacola News Journal* published a five-day series of articles called "Brownsville Revival: The Money and the Myths," calling revival-related businesses "a multimillion-dollar retail industry conducted within the walls of the church." The articles created a steady stream of charges and counter-charges, a lengthy list of accusations and denials, and a mountain of paper, including statements from attorneys, accountants, and auditors.

On Sunday, June 21, 1997, while Brownsville members were celebrating the revival's third anniversary, the *News Journal* published the first installment of its second investigative series, "Brownsville Revival: The Money and the Myths, Part II." While the four-day series failed to find any smoking guns, it did report that attendance at the revival had decreased slightly, even though money continued to flow into the coffers of the church and the pockets of the revival's leaders.

Using every document he could get his hands on, one of the paper's reporters estimated that the revival had brought in between 4.3 million and 5.4 million dollars in donations and sales in 1996. But by this time, revival leaders were declining the paper's requests for interviews. That, combined with their reluctance to release key financial documents, only made it look to many readers that they had something to hide.

Brownsville leaders admit that mistakes have been made, but they deny any legal or ethical wrongdoing. And in this case, as in most other similar cases, no amount of sleuthing or snooping can reveal the truth about the secret motives of ministry leaders. Only God knows the hidden things of the human heart.

But if movies about ministries are any indication of public

opinion, there is a presumption of guilt when it comes to God's servants.

Film Flimflam

Take a bit of Aimee Semple McPherson, the charismatic and controversial evangelist whose Angelus Temple in Los Angeles would become the birthplace of the International Church of the Foursquare Gospel denomination. Next, add a bit of Billy Sunday, the popular baseball-player-turned-pulpiteer whose sermons featured off-color saloon stories, hilarious vaudeville antics, and unrestrained theatricality. Mix the ingredients well, heat under cameras and spotlights, and voilà: you've got *Elmer Gantry*, the multiple-Oscar-winning 1960 film that gave movie-goers an over-the-top look at the religion racket.

Still as entertaining—and frightening—today as it was nearly four decades ago, the film is based on the 1927 novel by Sinclair Lewis, an outspoken social critic and muckraking writer. Teaming the sanctified sultriness of Sister Sharon Falconer, a fictional female revivalist, with the hard-driving hucksterism of a cynical con man (with the title role being played by Burt Lancaster, who won an Oscar for his riveting performance), *Elmer Gantry* is not only a genuine American film classic, but also a kind of Rorschach test of all those things that make people feel slightly queasy about revivalism.

The film has all the makings of a controversial best-seller: sex scandals; nosy reporters; high-pressure requests for money; superstar celebrity preachers; high-powered advance men; simple, straightforward, and emotionally affecting gospel messages; urgent exhortations about the unprecedented decline in American morals; suspicious and disapproving establishment-type pastors (who at one point are shown debating whether they should "marry the church to a three-ring circus"); and thousands upon thousands of gullible, spiritually hungry people.

Elmer Gantry also presents an inside look at revival leaders who would rather drown in their own sin and moral relativism than submit to the accountability or discipline of any external board or denomination. "What is a revival?" asks reporter Jim Lefferts, while phoning in the latest in his series of news stories about Sister Falconer and Brother Gantry.

> Is it a church? Is it a religion? Or is it a circus sideshow complete with freaks, magic and rabble-rousing? . . .
>
> [And] what qualifies someone to be a revivalist? Nothing. Nothing at all.

But it is not only fictional treatments of revivalism that have raised doubts about the whole revival enterprise. At least two powerful documentaries have attempted to capture real-life religious shenanigans. *The Disappearance of Aimee*, a relatively well-done 1976 made-for-TV film, raised questions about McPherson's controversial 1926 absence. The evangelist claimed she had been abducted, but just about everybody else believed she had run off with her radio manager, David Ormiston, the man who was to become her third husband.

And *Marjoe*, which won a 1972 Oscar for Best Feature Documentary, was once popular on college campuses and at art theaters, where it only confirmed its viewers' worst suspicions about evangelists. Based on the life of Marjoe Gortner, a little-known child evangelist, the film shows how a drink-, drug-, and sex-crazed Marjoe can still go through the motions and frisk his flocks long after he has abandoned the very faith he preaches so powerfully.

Most of the time, however, films about revival flimflam have focused on fictional characters like Jonas Nightengale, played by Steve Martin in the popular 1992 film, *Leap of Faith*. Martin turns in a less-than-convincing performance as a traveling tent preacher. But like *Elmer Gantry*, there are aspects of the film that are based on real life.

As he walks through his tent and looks at members of his audience, Nightengale receives information about some of them. But this is not, as he claims, a revelation from God. Instead, his able assistant (played by Debra Winger) gathers the information from ushers and then transmits it to Nightengale through a tiny receiver hidden in the evangelist's ear.

Such techniques may sound outlandish, but they were perfected by real-life evangelist Peter Popoff and his wife during the 1980s. Unfortunately for them, some of their transmissions were picked up by hoax buster James "The Amazing" Randi, who took a radio scanner to a Popoff crusade. Randi exposed Popoff on nationwide television. Prior to that, the evangelist's ministry had been bringing in four million dollars a year. Following Randi's exposé, Popoff filed for bankruptcy in 1987. But now Popoff is back on the air, proving that either God—or the TV-watching public—is very forgiving.

There is not enough space to cover anti-evangelist and anti-revivalist films like *Glory! Glory!*, *Preacherman*, *Salvation!*, *Invasion of the Space Preachers*, or two separate (and mediocre) TV movies from the early 1980s entitled *Pray TV*, one starring Dabney Coleman and the other with Ned Beatty.

The profusion of anti-evangelist films may suggest that Hollywood harbors deep resentment toward religious firebrands who routinely blast its entertainment products as evil. But such movies also reveal that there is a deep-seated suspicion about the financial trappings of Christianity, a suspicion that has dogged the church for centuries.

Money Troubles

From the beginning, the church has urged people to give their hearts to God and their earthy possessions to His designated representatives.

In the fourth chapter of the book of Acts, we see a picture of the radical Christian communalism of those who were a part of the early church. "Now the multitude of those who believed were of one heart and one soul; neither did anyone say that any of the things he possessed was his own, but they had all things in common" (v. 32).

The fifth chapter of Acts shows what happened to Ananias and Sapphira, a couple who sold some of their worldly goods but held back a portion of the proceeds from the brethren. Both "fell down and breathed [their] last" after God exposed their dishonesty. "So great fear came upon all the church and upon all who heard these things" (v. 11).

A millennium later, this primitive Christian communalism had been replaced by a massive Roman Catholic bureaucracy, but the fear was still there, only now it was fanned by official church representatives who raised money for the Crusades by selling indulgences. Think of indulgences as "Get Out of Hell Free" cards, which applied the spiritual capital of deceased saints to the deficits of living believers. By 1517, when Martin Luther wrote his Ninety-Five Theses, the sale of indulgences— now used to fund massive church building projects—had become a horrible abuse, which Luther singled out as a glaring example of the need for reform.

Although the Reformation brought an end to Roman Catholic hegemony, it did not put an end to Christianity's money troubles. And in America, where revivalism flourished, financial irregularities dogged some of the preachers now regarded as heroes of the faith.

In addition to coaxing sinners to repent, George Whitefield, the renowned evangelist of the first Great Awakening, could convince people to part with much of their cash. Benjamin Franklin, who was a friend and business associate of Whitefield's, apparently never gave his soul to Jesus, but he did give the silver-tongued evangelist some of his money. "He made large collections," recalled Franklin, "for his eloquence had a wonderful power over the hearts and purses of his hearers." Franklin described one particular instance when Whitefield's powers overcame Franklin's resistance:

> I had in my pocket a handful of copper money, three or four silver dollars, and five pistoles in gold. As he proceeded I began to soften, and concluded to give the coppers. Another stroke of his oratory made me ashamed of that, and determined me to give the silver; and he finished so admirably that I emptied my pocket wholly into the collector's dish, gold and all.

Contemporary church historian Mark Noll praises Whitefield for his integrity, saying: "Whitefield never kept money for himself beyond what he needed for the bare necessities. He never bought the eighteenth-century equivalent of a Mercedes or a summer home in the Bahamas."

But in his own day, Whitefield came in for harsh criticism for the way he handled his finances. During his first American preaching tour in 1738, he devoted significant amounts of money to help the poor and educate the young in Georgia. Later Whitefield founded an orphanage for troubled boys near Savannah, which he called "Bethesda," or "House of Mercy." Problems developed almost immediately. Some critics questioned the wisdom of creating a charity in such a remote location.

Disagreements later surfaced between Whitefield and his trustees, who withdrew their support from the venture. But that wasn't all: a wealthy benefactor died without leaving anything for Bethesda in his will; a shipment of supplies on its way to the orphanage was stolen; and Whitefield faced the threat of jail if he did not make good on his financial pledges. "I am almost tempted to wish I had never undertaken the Orphan House," said a discouraged Whitefield. Only the generosity of a wealthy European donor released Whitefield from his obligations, and his gloom.

Although there is no evidence that Whitefield did anything illegal or immoral, his sad experiences with Bethesda cast a shadow of doubt over the career of an otherwise exemplary evangelist.

From Whitefield's time until our own, those who preach the gospel have routinely been tripped up by money troubles. And the leaders of the Brownsville revival are no different.

"This Isn't About Money"

It is a Saturday morning, and Michael Brown is speaking to hundreds of people in Brownsville's sanctuary about staying on fire for God. But before he launches into his talk on the subject, he lets his hearers know that buying revival-related books and products is one practical thing they can do to help them remain fervent.

"This is not a sales pitch," he says before delivering something that sure sounds like a sales pitch, "but let me encourage you to go out of here with as many materials you can travel with." Brown himself has written nearly a dozen books, some of which he holds up before the crowd. "I hate holding up book covers," he says, "but I might as well hold them all up. If you're here to criticize, you can take a nice picture."

One could use up a good quantity of film taking pictures of Brownsville revival leaders pitching products and taking up offerings.

Like many churches, Brownsville records its services and sells audio- and videotapes to those who want them. But when you have as many services and as many interested buyers as Brownsville does, that can be a ton of tapes.

Yet it doesn't stop there. The church's sixteen-page "Revival Product Catalog" lists praise and worship music recordings, books and sermons by Pastor John Kilpatrick and evangelist Steve Hill, assorted manuals on everything from intercessory prayer to ushers' procedures, T-shirts, bumper stickers, and even a six-dollar Brownsville tote bag to hold all your purchases.

People can take or leave these products, which for the first few years of revival were sold in the church's foyer before a separate facility was built for them on the church grounds in 1998. But there is less freedom of choice when it comes to pleas for offerings, which can come without warning and can last as long as half an hour each.

"We're not ashamed to take an offering," said Kilpatrick during one revival service, stating a fact that would not come as a surprise to anyone who has regularly attended the services.

Much of the time, offering duties are handled by Carey Robertson, Brownsville's assistant pastor, who could author a collection of colorful offering-themed illustrations. "All of us are designed to be pipes, not pots," he says at one point, urging his listeners to let money flow into the ushers' containers. On another day, when a lightning strike has temporarily knocked out some of the church's air conditioners, Robertson reminds revivalgoers that somebody has to pay for the electricity, carpet, and toilet paper that everyone seems to take for granted.

And when he finishes pleading with his hearers, Robertson often prays about the offering, which gives him a chance to plead with his hearers in a slightly different tone of voice. "God, we struggle with this matter of money in the church," he intones, "but people don't understand how you work. Jesus, while You were here on the earth, You talked about this all the time." Perhaps Robertson could have clarified that Jesus talked frequently about the evils of money, and never took up an offering for Himself. But that might have confused people, causing some to give less.

On Friday evenings, offerings taken up at revival services go to Steve Hill's Together in the Harvest Ministries, and Kilpatrick often does the fundraising honors for his partner and friend. "This revival is not about money," he said during one twenty-five-minute appeal for funds. "It never has been and never will be." Still, money is a recurring topic. "I know that Steve Hill could be bringing in a whole lot more money than he gets here, but this isn't about money."

Front-Page News

In September 1997 John Kilpatrick was taking a look at how construction was going on his new home when he fell off a ledge and landed hard about twenty feet below. He barely missed the jagged blade of a table saw and an uneven stairway, but he still broke eight ribs and tore up his pelvis in four places. He was in horrible pain, but was still glad to be alive.

It was while Kilpatrick was emerging from surgery and sedation that he first got the word: reporters from the *Pensacola News Journal* were snooping around his property. For the next two months, the snooping would continue as reporters from the *News Journal*, a small daily paper that had previously published dozens of mostly favorable articles about the revival, worked on the biggest investigative project in its history: a five-day series of nearly three dozen articles that set out to demonstrate that the revival was a sham. In addition to alleging that Kilpatrick was an ecclesiastical tyrant, that Hill was dishonest, and that the whole so-called revival had been planned and carried off by human effort, the series dealt at length with the issue of money, charging at one point that "revival leaders are making fortunes."

Specifically, the paper examined four nonprofit corporations created by four Brownsville revival leaders: Kilpatrick's Feast of Fire Ministries, Inc.; Hill's Together in the Harvest Ministries, Inc.; Brown's ICN Ministries, Inc.; and Music Missions International, Inc., founded by Brownsville worship leader Lindell Cooley. The paper found that none of these organizations were members of the Evangelical Council for Financial Accountability, a watchdog organization founded by Billy

Graham and other Christian leaders to promote financial integrity. Assemblies evangelists Bakker and Swaggart had not been members either. And as this book was going to press in late 1998, none of the Brownsville-related ministries had yet met the requirements for ECFA membership.

In fact, evangelicals and pentecostals seldom see eye-to-eye on money issues. Evangelicals and groups like ECFA emphasize external controls, full disclosure, and systems of accountability. Pentecostals more often talk about trust and just rewards. For example, pentecostal Pat Robertson's 1997 sale of his Family Channel to entertainment entrepreneur Rupert Murdoch had many evangelicals fuming, in part because Robertson had created his network from the tax-deductible contributions of faithful supporters. But when *Charisma* magazine published an article questioning the sale, its pentecostal and charismatic readers were unhappy. "Pat has worked hard writing books and speaking all over the world," wrote one reader. "God has blessed this man. Is there anything wrong with that?" Another said, "Don't people have anything better to do than criticize someone else? And I thought that *my* life was boring!"

In addition to not being members of ECFA, all four Brownsville revival-related ministries had sold hundreds of thousands of dollars' worth of products, but only Brown's ministry had paid any Florida sales taxes.

And that's not all. The Pensacola newspaper also charged that

- all of the ministries, except for Cooley's Music Missions International, declined to reveal revenue and spending details, and that Brownsville's Carey Robertson declared that such information was "nobody's business but ours."
- Kilpatrick's and Hill's ministries were giving less money to missions than each claimed, and that instead money was going to fund the two leaders' luxurious lifestyles;
- church officials requested that people give at least one hun-

dred dollars during several revival service offerings, and accepted gifts of expensive "articles of affection," including jewelry.

- Awake America rallies held in Anaheim, Dallas, St. Louis, Toledo, Birmingham, and Memphis netted even more funds for the four revival leaders, who organized the rallies through a separate organization, which was a joint venture with the Brownsville church.

ECFA president Paul Nelson, who read the newspaper's 1997 stories, deemed the allegations serious. "Some of the charges would give the impression that someone has benefited personally" from the revival, said Nelson, adding that ECFA guidelines are designed to prevent leaders from deriving personal benefits—other than fixed salary and compensation packages—from their ministries.

Revival leaders responded to the series with threats of lawsuits, demands for retractions, denunciations, and a series of rebuttals. "Everything in the reports that was scandalous was not true," said Brown, "and everything that was true was not scandalous."

Still, the lawsuits never materialized, and the retractions were never issued, as the paper stood behind its reports. Revival leaders also claim the newspaper lost numerous advertisers—a claim the paper denies.

The denunciations of the *News Journal's* series may have assured the faithful, who continued to attend revival services in record numbers. In addition, revival leaders distributed their rebuttals to news organizations, through the church's Web site, and in ads purchased by the church and published by the *News Journal*, but it's hard to tell if these efforts did much to erase people's suspicions.

Today Kilpatrick describes the whole episode as something akin to being taken to the woodshed for punishment. "I had my hiney whipped," he says.

I've never had an adversarial relationship with the press. I had no idea that I was supposed to tell them my salary. That was private information. I wasn't aware I needed to deal with them along those lines. But I've learned a good lesson.

And revival leaders say there have been other benefits to come out of the whole mess. Kilpatrick now reveals his Brownsville salary and benefits package (around seventy thousand dollars, which is less than that paid to some other area pastors). He has also agreed to take no more than one hundred thousand dollars a year in income from his own Feast of Fire ministry.

Offering pitches no longer include requests for hundred-dollar gifts. All four organizations have at least begun investigating membership in the ECFA. And all four ministries are now paying Florida sales taxes. (Attorney Larry Morris says that government officials had given conflicting and inconclusive answers to his questions about whether the ministries were required to pay sales taxes. Still, the three ministries that had not been paying any taxes prior to the publication of the *News Journal's* series delivered checks by the time the five-day series was completed.)

If there is a bright side to the whole story, it's that the *News Journal* reported in 1998 that Brownsville was taking significant strides toward more responsible financial accounting and reporting procedures.

There is no indication that anyone connected to Brownsville broke any laws or attempted to mislead anybody, and no government entities are conducting any official investigations. In addition, revival leaders say they have declined to become involved in numerous potentially lucrative projects that have been dangled before them, such as starting a regular TV show on the TBN network.

Hill admits that mistakes were made, but vehemently denies

the charge that anyone was being dishonest or crooked. "I admit that I am naive in some areas of ministry," he said. "I'm young. I've never been thrust into an area like this."

Certainly, the financial missteps made by the Brownsville revival leaders are not of Elmer Gantry caliber, and they may not even be as serious as the problems George Whitefield faced. Still, they caused the revival and its leaders to endure criticism, which could have been avoided if everyone involved had followed sound and established financial procedures.

Covering and Accountability

"Finances have always followed revival," says Assemblies of God General Superintendent Thomas Trask. "You don't have revival for finances, but they have always come as a result of revival."

When it became clear to Trask that the Brownsville revival was going to be around for a while, he organized a "covering committee," designed to provide guidance and accountability for revival leaders. Money has been just one of the topics the committee has discussed with Kilpatrick and Hill.

Trask believes that some of the *News Journal's* stories were unfair and misleading, and he has had his own difficulties getting straight answers from the IRS. But still, he doesn't think Kilpatrick helped matters by withholding financial information from the paper. Officially, the denomination leaves it up to each congregation to determine how much it will divulge and to whom, but Trask clearly believes that pastors ought to be open and forthcoming:

My philosophy has always been openness, and I've encouraged John [Kilpatrick] to be open. We are entrusted with people's trust, and for people to trust us there has to be an openness. There's nothing to hide, so why not tell them?

Kilpatrick now agrees that disclosure is the best policy. "I'm open," he says. "Wide open." And he has long believed in the importance of submission to his spiritual leaders, in this case Trask and other denominational leaders.

> I'm in total submission to brother Trask and the Assemblies of God, and if they pick up the phone and tell me they're real troubled about something, I'd put a lot of weight in that. That's the commitment I made to the denomination when I signed on the dotted line [at his ordination] in 1966. When a preacher can't listen to his superiors, he's too big for his britches.

Kilpatrick's commitment to accountability sets him apart not only from the fictional Gantry, but from real-life evangelists Bakker and Swaggart, who launched out on their own rather than submit to church discipline and guidance.

Still, some critics are not as troubled by financial misdeeds as they are by alleged theological errors. And it is the heated debates about the theology of revival that we will explore next.

Changed Lives

No more hypocrisy

Walter Spivey used to praise God on Sundays and go bar-hopping the rest of the week. Now he's sold out on serving God.

"God Did a Big Thing to Me"

Walter Spivey was living a double life. On Sunday mornings he sang and played drums with the choir at Tabernacle of Faith in Stockton, California. But the rest of the time, he could care less about God, as his actions outside of church plainly revealed.

"My spiritual life was way twisted," he recalls. "I would sleep with my girlfriend as well as other girls, party at clubs, and do a little drinking and smoking now and then. I was open to anything out there."

Walter was so accustomed to religious hypocrisy—both in his life and the lives of those around him—that he openly ridiculed God. "I would see people shake and fall at church, but then they would get up and go back to doing the same things they did before they got into the Spirit," he says. "At parties, my friends and I would mock God. I would 'pray' for my friend, and he would fall down. And then he would 'pray' for me, and I would fall. It was sick."

When he turned twenty-one, Walter set his sights on Florida. He wanted to celebrate his birthday in "all the big clubs I had seen on TV." But reality was not as exciting as his fantasies. "When I got down there, I was a wreck. It was horrible."

Back home in Stockton, Walter saw a big change in his pastor and his pastor's wife. The two had visited the Brownsville revival, where they were touched by God. When they invited a group of young people to go back to Brownsville with them, Walter tentatively agreed. After the sermon, Walter went down to the altar to repent of his sins. But as soon as he got back to California, he was back to his old ways.

His pastor finally got fed up with Walter and other hypocrites, disbanding the church's choir and worship team, and focusing on repentance and seeking God. "I gave my life to the Lord," says Walter.

"I even gave my girlfriend away. She meant a whole lot to me, and breaking up with her was a real tragedy. But I knew I was going to spend eternity with Jesus, and that made everything better."

Next, Walter began asking God to use him. "I prayed, 'Lord, please put me in a college where I can get away from my friends and fulfill Your goals for my life.'" About the same time, Walter's pastor returned from a visit to Pensacola, where he had been touched by the revival. As Walter heard his pastor describe the Brownsville Revival School of Ministry, which would be opening soon, he says he "knew immediately in my spirit that it was God's will for me to go there."

That conviction has only grown stronger during Walter's time at the school. "Before I came here I didn't know nothing," he says. "I couldn't even quote John 3:16. But now my walk with the Lord is growing deeper. And so is my passion to see other people come to the Lord."

Walter believes God is calling him to the ministry, but so far, he's not sure if he will be a pastor, an evangelist, a missionary, or something else.

"I have a desire to preach the gospel. If the Lord puts me in a convalescent home washing toilets and witnessing to people, that would be fine. All I know is that God has me here for a purpose. I'm not supposed to come here for six months and be the next Billy Graham. I'm supposed to be here for two years and then do what He wants."

In the meantime, Walter remains amazed at the changes that have happened in his life.

"God did a big thing for me," he says, smiling broadly. "If you could see where I used to be before, and where I am now, you could see that it's a miracle."

Worship at Brownsville is often exuberant and emotional. That's how revival has always been, leading critics to ask if people are putting heart over mind, or worse.

CHAPTER ELEVEN

Testing the Spirits:

Debating the Theology of Revival

For true believers, the Brownsville revival is a wonderful and miraculous thing, and an important part of God's supernatural efforts to renew and revive the body of Christ. But skeptics view what is happening in Brownsville as bogus and potentially dangerous.

Although he is far from the only critic of Brownsville, Hank Hanegraaff is one of the most vocal. As president of the California-based Christian Research Institute and host of the organization's daily "Bible Answer Man" radio broadcast, Hanegraaff has urged believers to heed the warning found in the first epistle of John: "Beloved, do not believe every spirit, but test the spirits, whether they are of God" (4:1). As he writes in his latest best-selling book:

This warning is particularly relevant today, as Christianity is undergoing a paradigm shift of major proportions—a shift from faith to feelings, from fact to fantasy, and from reason to esoteric revelation. This paradigm shift is what I call the Counterfeit Revival.

How can such strong disagreements arise among Christian believers? The answer can be found in the subtle but profound theological differences that divide one believer from another. For centuries, revival has brought such glaring differences into sharp contrast. And in some ways, today's often heated debates about Brownsville are not that different from the controversy that surrounded evangelist George Whitefield.

Revival Rancor

Today Whitefield is hailed as a hero of the faith and honored as a key figure in the famous Great Awakening. But in his own day, Whitefield was criticized and condemned on both sides of the Atlantic.

The subject of both ribald songs and satirical plays, Whitefield saw his theology attacked in numerous pamphlets, and the evangelist's controversial practice of preaching to people in large outdoor gatherings made him a regular target of angry mobs.

Whitefield also came under fire from John Wesley, a dear brother in Christ who had worked closely with Whitefield in England before the two men parted ways over a number of issues, including the theology of free will. Whitefield was a Calvinist who believed that God ultimately ordained who would be saved. Wesley was an Arminian who criticized Whitefield publicly in a 1739 sermon. Wesley defended the concept of "free grace," arguing that God's saving mercies were available to all, not just to those "whom God hath ordained."

Further, Wesley thundered that Whitefield's doctrine portrayed "our blessed Lord . . . as a hypocrite, a deceiver of the people, a man void of common sincerity." A year and a half later, Whitefield reluctantly responded to Wesley's accusations in a thirty-one-page pamphlet, writing, "For Christ's sake be not rash! Give yourself to reading. Study the covenant of grace. Down with your carnal reasoning."

Whitefield and Wesley later reconciled personally, although

they never saw eye-to-eye on doctrine. Instead, they agreed to disagree for the rest of their lives. While their friendship never recovered the intimacy and warmth it had before their falling out, the two were able to lay aside much of the acrimony that had characterized their fighting years.

There was no warmth, however, between New England minister Charles Chauncy and Whitefield. Chauncy, for sixty years the pastor of Boston's imposing First Church, shared Wesley's disagreement with the Great Awakening's Calvinistic theology. In addition, he had a total distaste for the revival's emotionalism. For Chauncy, who was perhaps the revival's most outspoken critic, the Great Awakening was not so great.

In 1742 Jonathan Edwards wrote a sympathetic account of the Awakening in his work, *Some Thoughts Concerning the Present Revival of Religion in New England.* In 1743 Chauncy responded with his own work *Seasonable Thoughts on the State of Religion.* In that work and in many of his sermons, Chauncy attacked and ridiculed the unbridled enthusiasm of the revival. A rationalist, Chauncy argued that religion was more concerned with reason than emotion. To him, Christianity was a matter of established creeds and rituals, not dramatic personal experiences or distinctive encounters with God.

In his *Seasonable Thoughts,* Chauncy set out to give an accurate account of "the many and great Mistakes of the present Day," most of which involved people's deception about their own religious experiences. "They are ready, at once, if [something] is unusual, or strong, to take it for some Influence from above," he wrote, declaring that such deception is demonic:

Nay, what Engine has the Devil himself ever made Use of, to more fatal Purposes, in all Ages, than the Passions of the Vulgar heightened to such a Degree, as to put them upon acting without Thought and Understanding? The plain Truth is, an enlightened Mind, and not raised affections.

A Chorus of Criticism

From Chauncy in the mid-eighteenth century to Hanegraaff at the end of the twentieth, a chorus of criticism has accompanied every alleged outbreak of spiritual awakening. In the last chapter we discussed the criticism that has accompanied revivalism's outright quacks, charlatans, and frauds. But in this chapter, we will examine the heated debates over the very theology of revival, debates that have divided believers for centuries.

Over the years, four major areas have been the cause of most of the recurring theological critiques leveled against revivals.

Unusual Manifestations

Revivals have long been renowned for their emotionalism and the passionate outbursts they inspire. John Wesley, for example, noted in a 1759 journal entry how hearers reacted to the preaching of one evangelist:

> Some of those who were here pricked to the heart, were affected in an astonishing manner. The first man I saw wounded would have dropped, but others, catching him in their arms, did indeed, prop him up, but were so far from keeping him still, that he caused all of them to totter and tremble. His own shaking exceeded that of a cloth in the wind. It seemed as if the Lord came upon him like a giant, taking him by the neck, and shaking all his bones in pieces.

Similar outbursts are regular occurrences at Brownsville. Cathy Wood is a church member who has been involved in the revival from the beginning. She has also documented the revival in regular written reports and photographs. In fact, it is her photos that appear on the cover and on the inside of this book.

In 1997 Cathy produced a self-published book called *The*

Visitation, which includes some of her reports and many of her photos. Although she is not an official representative of Brownsville Assembly of God or the revival, her account, which includes numerous descriptions of the manifestations that have accompanied the revival, provides one insider's view of Brownsville's intense spiritual dynamics.

At one point, Cathy describes how she "became completely unconscious" as Steve Hill prayed for her and other worshipers. "I stayed in a woozy condition all the time," she writes. Later, as church members told each other what God had done for them during the revival, "we would all have our heads shaking or jerking as we talked about the Lord." During one revival service, Cathy says she experienced angelic sounds, a blue haze around the ceiling of the church, and a glorious fragrance. "It is like being swept away in a large swift current in a river or being washed over by a wave in the ocean," she wrote. She did not remember much about another service: "I wish I could tell more, but I kept going in and out."

Such experiences may have seemed normal within the confines of the church, but sometimes the jerking revival-goers experienced at church continued after they left, which contributed to some unique visits to the grocery store, or curious glances from next-door neighbors. "I wonder what our neighbors must think when they see us after a service," she writes. "We leave home all neat and pressed and return with hair in disarray, shirts half untucked, and walking funny."

Such goings-on concern Hanegraaff, who says he is "gravely concerned about the spiritual and physical consequences of unbiblical manifestations such as spasmodic jerking and being 'slain in the spirit.'" To Hanegraaff, such behaviors seem to have little to do with God and are more likely due to peer pressure, the power of suggestion, and "the old and pervasive principles of hypnotism."

Overemphasis on Manifestations

For some critics it is not manifestations themselves that are the problem but rather an overemphasis on them.

Chaotic services are nearly as old as the faith itself. The early Christian believers in Corinth were exceptionally exuberant, and their often chaotic worship services eventually required the calming influence of the apostle Paul, who wrote: "Therefore, brethren, desire earnestly to prophesy, and do not forbid to speak in tongues. Let all things be done decently and in order" (1 Cor. 14:39–40).

Ask contemporary believers what the words "decently and in order" mean, and you'll hear a dizzying variety of responses, many of them seemingly derived more from people's upbringing and socialization than from theological principles. Some are fine with tears but draw the line at uncontrolled sobbing. Others are fine with upraised hands, but recoil at swaying or dancing. Many would probably express discomfort with jerking, moaning, or falling in the Spirit—all of which were common manifestations during the Great Awakening. More extravagant manifestations—such as people barking like dogs or crowing like roosters—accompanied the frontier camp meetings of the Second Great Awakening, as well as the so-called Toronto or "Holy Laughter" revival.

The behavior of some Toronto worshipers has troubled many observers, who say some of its services have been characterized by a circuslike atmosphere where strange behaviors and gyrations are given more attention than the comparatively mundane message of the gospel. Another danger is that unusual manifestations will be seen as some kind of litmus test used to measure the truthfulness and depth of people's faith. Many believers who love God deeply but never express that affection with bold, bodily manifestations would sadly fail any such test.

Putting Heart over Head

Other critics are fine with extravagant displays of affection for God. What bothers them is the tendency for revival fervor to lead people into theological error, replacing the objective authority of Scripture with subjective experiences, mystical leadings, new revelations, or an overemphasis on prophecy and "words of wisdom."

History shows there is good reason to be concerned. During the early days of the Azusa Street revival, for example, alleged incidents of spiritism, hypnotism, and various fleshly and even demonic outbreaks caused a permanent conflict between revival leader William Seymour and his mentor, Charles Parham, who was barred from preaching at or even attending any more revival services.

And in the decade after the Azusa Street revival, as many as one-fifth of the nation's pentecostals dispensed with orthodox theology about the Trinity, in part as a result of what they claimed were new revelations from God. These believers espoused the view that Jesus, God, and the Holy Spirit were in actuality one person, whose name was Jesus; and they insisted that people who had previously been baptized in the name of the Father, the Son, and the Holy Spirit be rebaptized in the name of Jesus only. Booted out of the Assemblies of God and other pentecostal denominations for their heresy, some of these "Jesus only" or "oneness" believers sought solace in a variety of splinter groups before uniting in 1945 under the banner of the United Pentecostal Church.

Few would claim that doctrinal errors like these always accompany powerful outbreaks of revival fervor. Still, the tragedy of believers yielding to "new prophecies" and embracing heresy does not have to be common to be condemned. And while no major leaders have accused Brownsville's leaders of heresy, Hanegraaff has charged them with "serious distortions of biblical Christianity."

Upsetting the Applecart

Over the centuries a host of questions and criticisms have been raised concerning revival's unsettling impact on a wide range of religious, social, and cultural traditions.

For example, revivals have had a profound leveling effect in the church, in some cases empowering and unleashing laypeople to perform tasks such as evangelism and intercession, which were previously thought to be the sole prerogative of the clergy, and in other cases calling women to perform tasks once believed to be restricted to men.

In addition, revivals have often demolished long-entrenched social rules and routines. The Azusa Street revival, which was started by an African-American man, led to intermingling of whites and blacks on a scale that was shocking to many at the dawn of the twentieth century. Azusa's multicultural melting-pot approach still influences pentecostal churches today. Pentecostal and charismatic congregations routinely exhibit a much more racially integrated fellowship than either evangelical or mainstream Protestant churches, many of which remain some of the most segregated institutions in contemporary American life.

There is also a sense in which revival routinely subverts sacrosanct socioeconomic conventions. Whitefield, who took his lumps for preaching to the masses in the open air, regularly preached to the rich and powerful as well. But there were some among the elite who found his commitment to evangelize both groups "repulsive." The countess of Buckingham, for one, was critical of what she considered Whitefield's efforts

> to level all ranks and do away with all distinctions. It is monstrous to be told that you have a heart as sinful as the common

wretches that crawl upon the earth. This is highly offensive and insulting . . . so much at variance with high rank and good breeding.

Revival also wreaks havoc on established denominational boundaries and distinctives. Azusa Street gave birth to hundreds of new denominations, while the charismatic movement and the Jesus movement of the 1960s and 1970s ushered in profound changes in the ways Christians fellowshiped and worshiped together. And at Brownsville, evangelist Steve Hill is an unabashed nondenominationalist, saying in one sermon, "As I read the Bible, I don't find denominations, only disciples."

In short, there is plenty about revival and its consequences to rattle traditionalists, who typically view their traditions as divinely ordained, and who usually view any and all attempts to change things as nothing less than subverting godly order and authority. For such people, revival nearly always spells disruption, dismay, and the end of Christianity-as-usual.

Defender of the Faith

The Christian Research Institute was founded in 1960 by pioneering cult researcher and apologist Walter Martin, who devoted his life to researching and teaching about cults and non-Christian religious movements. Martin, a serious scholar who held four earned degrees, came out with the first edition of his now-classic *The Kingdom of the Cults* in 1965, and it has regularly been revised and reprinted ever since.

The book, like most of Martin's labors, focused solely on doctrines and groups that were clearly opposed to Christian teaching, including centuries-old faiths like Hinduism and Islam, as well as newer non-Christian groups like Mormonism and Scientology. Martin's focus on cults and "-isms" did not include pentecostalism, except for rare criticisms of the so-called Word-Faith movement, which he believed was theologically flawed.

But under the leadership of Hank Hanegraaff, who has been CRI's president since Martin's death in 1989, the ministry—which bills itself as "The Pentagon of Apologetics"—has increasingly turned its guns on fellow believers.

Hanegraaff's best-selling 1993 book, *Christianity in Crisis,* received a Gold Medallion Award from the Evangelical Christian Publishers Association. It attacked the excesses of the Faith Movement, along with its pentecostal, neo-pentecostal, and charismatic leaders, including Kenneth Hagin, Kenneth Copeland, Benny Hinn, Marilyn Hickey, Paul Crouch, and others. As he wrote in the book's introduction:

> If cultic and occultic systems like the New Age movement pose the greatest threat to the body of Christ from without, the deadly cancer represented by [the Faith Movement] poses one of the greatest threats to Christianity from within.

As Hanegraaff saw it, "multitudes are being duped by a gospel of greed and are embracing doctrines straight from the metaphysical cults," and as a result, "Christianity is hurtling at breakneck speed into a crisis of unparalleled proportions."

Hanegraaff's 1997 book, *Counterfeit Revival,* was published by Word, which is a division of Thomas Nelson, publisher of the book you are reading right now. *Counterfeit Revival,* which could have been called *Christianity in Crisis: The Sequel,* went after John Wimber's Vineyard association of churches—focusing particular attention on the Toronto Airport Vineyard, site of one of the most dramatic demonstrations of the so-called "Laughing Revival"—and attacked many of the worst excesses of contemporary charismatic Christianity.

Christianity Today published a scathing review of the book by theologian James Beverly, who called it "a misleading, simplistic, and harmful book, marred by faulty logic, outdated and limited research, and nasty misrepresentation of key charismatic leaders." Hanegraaff responded in a letter to the magazine that Beverly was not exactly an objective critic, since "he self-publishes materials in support of counterfeit revivalists." And in a response to the review published in his own ministry's magazine, Hanegraaff complained about Beverly's use of "shrill and sarcastic language" and the review's use of "words like 'simplistic.'"

It may surprise some people that Hanegraaff's book does not even mention Brownsville. Only on page 244 of the 252-page text does he make a passing reference to "pastors and parishioners [who] are traveling to 'power centers' like Toronto, Canada, and Pensacola, Florida, looking for a quick fix."

But by the time of his April 1997 appearance on CNN's *Larry King Live,* Hanegraaff had Brownsville in his crosshairs, telling a nationwide television audience that the Brownsville revival shared similarities with the Heaven's Gate cult, which was the subject of King's show. For those who wondered how Heaven's Gate—a group whose thirty-nine most loyal members had taken their own lives so they could connect with a UFO—could be compared to Brownsville's pentecostal revival, Hanegraaff charged that both depended on "psychosocial manipulation" and fostered "altered states of consciousness."

Through most of the rest of 1997, Hanegraaff continued to hammer away at Brownsville through every medium he had at his disposal, including the audiotape version of *Counterfeit Revival;* his "Bible Answer Man" broadcasts; and in his ministry's magazine, *Christian Research Journal,* which published a series of four articles on "Counterfeit Revival." While some of these articles relied on material found in Hanegraaff's book, the third in the series, "Separating Fact from Fabrication on the Pensacola Outpouring," which appeared in the journal's November-December 1997 issue, used material that had not been previously published. It was in this article that Hanegraaff charged that the Brownsville revival's leaders were guilty of "serious distortions of biblical Christianity . . . an overemphasis on subjective experience . . . nonbiblical spiritual practices, Scripture twisting, and false and exaggerated claims."

In his epilogue to his *Counterfeit Revival* book, Hanegraaff spelled out what Christians needed to do in order to turn away from counterfeit revival to the real thing. "Church leaders must once again produce in their people a holy hunger for the Word of God," he writes. And instead of "looking for experience in all the wrong places," people should focus on "having an encounter with the Word of God. That's what makes the change [in a person's life]."

Defender of Revival

If Hanegraaff is one of Brownsville's most outspoken critics, it is Michael Brown, president of the Brownsville Revival School of Ministry, who serves as the revival's main defender. In his 1997 book, *Let No One Deceive You: Confronting the Critics of Revival*, Brown took on Hanegraaff and others who he believes have thrown out the baby with the baptismal water.

One of Brown's major points is that critics confuse Brownsville with other movements that are more feelings-oriented and less biblically based. Brownsville, says Brown, is a "repentance-based, evangelistically driven, holiness-stressing revival." Although he readily admits that Brownsville worshipers often exhibit enthusiasm and emotionalism, he argues that such activities are a result of the revival's ministry, not the central focus. And anyway, he says, the Bible does not teach against such things.

As for Hanegraaff's *Counterfeit Revival*, Brown calls it "an unscholarly, often inaccurate, highly judgmental, and at times, even slanderous work." Brown, who has numerous degrees, points out that Hanegraaff has none, and he asks what it is that qualifies Hanegraaff to speak as an authority on revival. "Just because you warn people about deception does not mean that you are not deceived," he writes.

Brown is zealous, but he says he is not so single-minded that he dismisses constructive criticism. Instead, he says he makes a distinction between criticism that is designed to be helpful and criticism that is merely destructive and malicious. He puts most of Hanegraaff's public comments about Brownsville in the latter category. "When criticism is so destructive and wrong-spirited, it's difficult to hear anything helpful out of it."

Brown has even less patience for people who attack the revival without ever seeing it in person. "God is moving in a sacred way. Lives are being deeply impacted. There's a ray of hope in the hearts of many. And others, some of whom don't even bother to come, are spewing out ugly opinions and baseless accusations."

Still, Brown does not expect revival to be calm and peaceful.

In *Let No One Deceive You,* he demonstrates from history that controversy and conflict accompany any spiritual awakening. Controversy cannot be avoided, he writes, because "revival, by definition and nature, will always be too loud for the lukewarm and too heavy for the halfhearted."

Finally, Brown urges critics to spend less time pointing fingers at believers in Brownsville and elsewhere and spend more time praying to God for true renewal. "If you are so convinced that the current revival is really a great deception, why not give yourself unceasingly to prayer and fasting for the real visitation you claim is still to come."

From Diatribe to Dialogue

In November 1997 Brown the defender and Hanegraaff the critic met face-to-face at a private dialogue organized by executives of the Salem Radio Network. Then in December, Hanegraaff—who had visited Brownsville four or five times before—went to Pensacola again, only this time he met with Brown, evangelist Steve Hill, and pastor John Kilpatrick. He spoke to students at Brown's school, where he received a warm reception and a standing ovation. Kilpatrick even invited Hanegraaff to preach at one of Brownsville's Sunday services, an offer Hanegraaff told me he was considering.

Following Hanegraaff's visit, the rumor mill went into overdrive. Some unofficial reports even stated that Hanegraaff had been slain in the spirit and began speaking in tongues. In a statement he issues to "set the record straight," Hanegraaff said he was "thrilled by the dialogue that is taking place," but emphasized that his visit to Brownsville "should not be interpreted as an endorsement of the 'Pensacola Outpouring.'"

One thing everyone agreed on was that the dialogue provided an opportunity for both sides to cool their tempers and quiet their nasty rhetoric. "One of the things we wanted to model was that we could discuss these things in a manner that would honor Christ instead of a way that would drag His name through the mud," Hanegraaff told me.

Brown says he and Hanegraaff emerged from their talks sharing common views on at least three points: "That we are brothers who are going to spend eternity together; that we are passionate for the fundamentals of the faith; and that we want to see disciples, not just converts."

Like Wesley and Whitefield, Brown and Hanegraaff have reconciled personally, but they continue to agree to disagree. Hanegraaff continues to criticize Brownsville, although less harshly than he did in the past. And Brown continues to defend the revival, arguing that believers tend to put contemporary revivals under a microscope, but they often look upon past revivals through rose-colored glasses. "We tend to sanitize past revivals and demonize present revivals," he says.

Will the Real Jonathan Edwards Please Stand Up?

When arguments break out over the theology of revival, Jonathan Edwards is often called on to referee the dispute. Edwards is widely regarded as one of the towering figures of American evangelicalism. Twentieth-century historian Perry Miller called Edwards "the greatest philosopher–theologian yet to grace the American scene." Centuries after his death Edwards's sermons are still regarded as classics of American literature. And he was both an avid participant and keen observer of the First Great Awakening.

Edwards's stature, combined with the fact that the Bible gives no details about what revival should look like, means that his works are eagerly scavenged by revival critics and supporters alike. Quotes from Edwards's books are wrenched out of context and employed by both sides as if they were some kind of *Good Housekeeping* seal of approval. And perhaps it is not surprising that opposing factions in the revival wars present differing pictures of who Edwards was and what he thought.

One of the best things people interested in revival could do is to put this book down and read Edwards for themselves. His 1741 work, *The Distinguishing Marks of a Work of the True Spirit,* which can be found in Banner of Truth's excellent 160-page collection, *Jonathan Edwards on Revival,* is a classic. Its prose still sings after two-and-a-half centuries, revealing a mind that is lively, deep, and brimming over with practical wisdom.

After quoting John's exhortation to "test the spirits," Edwards devotes the first section of his work to explaining his own method for testing the fruits of revival. Here Edwards explores something he called "negative signs." As Edwards explains, the nine negative signs he describes are "no signs by which we are to judge of a work." In other words, the criteria he describes should not be used to discredit a revival and declare that it is not from God.

For example, suppose people who have been touched by God during a so-called revival fall away into "gross errors, or scandalous practices" (Edwards's eighth negative sign). Edwards argues that such failings do not mean a revival is not from God.

Revivals that exhibit these nine signs may be of God, or they may not. Only God knows for sure. But Edwards's point is that observers should not rush to judgment and conclude that the presence of one or more of these signs proves that a revival is not of God. Edwards devoted twenty pages to a careful examination of the nine negative signs. The best we can do here is list them:

1. Nothing can be certainly concluded from this, That a work is carried on in a way very unusual and extraordinary; provided the variety or difference be such, as may still be comprehended within the limits of Scripture rules.

2. A work is not to be judged of by any effects on the bodies of men; such as tears, trembling, groans, loud outcries, agonies of body, or the failing of bodily strength.

3. It is no argument that an operation on the minds of people is not the work of the Spirit of God that it occasions a great deal of noise about religion.

4. It is no argument that an operation on the minds of a people is not the work of the Spirit of God that many who are the subjects of it have great impressions made on their imaginations.

5. It is no sign that a work is not from the Spirit of God that example is a great means of it . . . [By "example," Edwards meant the use of personal testimonies, a practice that he supported.]

6. It is no sign that a work is not from the Spirit of God that many who seem to be the subjects of it are guilty of great imprudences and irregularities in their conduct.

7. Nor are many errors in judgment, and some delusions of

Satan intermixed with the work, any argument that the work in general is not of the Spirit of God . . .

8. If some who were thought to be wrought upon [Edwards's lingo for "touched by God"] fall away into gross errors, or scandalous practices, it is no argument that the work in general is not the work of the Spirit of God.

9. It is no argument that a work is not from the Spirit of God that it seems to be promoted by ministers insisting very much on the terrors of God's holy law, and that with a great deal of pathos and earnestness.

Both Hanegraaff and Brown appeal to these signs. But in *Counterfeit Revival*, Edwards's nine negative signs become Hanegraaff's nine positive signs. In other words, things that Edwards argued could not be used to judge a revival are used to do just that. In Hanegraaff's hands, Edwards's non-signs become "signs" that provide "a clear demarcation between the Great Awakening and great apostasy." Or as Brown correctly puts it, Hanegraaff "proceeds to use these nine signs for the exact opposite purpose" intended by Edwards.

Reading Hanegraaff and other revival critics, a picture of Edwards emerges that portrays him as a staunch revival critic. Hanegraaff argues that if Edwards were alive today, he would be a harsh judge of contemporary "counterfeit revivals." And he charges that those who differ with this interpretation are engaging in "revisionary history," saying that they

appeal to one of the leading figures in American revivalism, Jonathan Edwards, to prove that the bizarre behaviors and extra-biblical revelations of their own "revival" are signs of an authentic work of God. Edwards did describe unusual manifestations that accompanied conversions during the First Great Awakening, but the great New England theologian was actually one of the most eloquent critics the church has ever seen of the principles and practices that characterize the Counterfeit Revival.

Further, Hanegraaff says Edwards claimed that the "peculiarities of wild enthusiasts" brought an end to the Great Awakening.

Reading Brown and other revival supporters, however, one gets a completely different perspective on Edwards and his views. In books like *Let No One Deceive You*, one finds that it is Hanegraaff who is guilty of "the misuse of Edwards's material to suit his own purposes." Brown charges that Hanegraaff is not a defender of the faith, but rather is a scoffer and a skeptic. "While claiming to follow in the footsteps of Jonathan Edwards, he has instead distinguished himself as the Charles Chauncy of this generation."

Unfortunately, Edwards is not here to defend himself, explain his views, or apply them to current revivals. But as I read Edwards, one of his main messages seems to be that revival can be very, very messy; but messiness, in itself, does not mean God is not in it.

A similar sentiment was expressed by John Wesley, who made this humble and earnest prayer to God: "Lord, if it please thee, work the same work again, without blemishes. But if that may not be, though it be with all the blemishes, work the same work."

One of the major lessons one finds in the writings of Edwards, Wesley, and other esteemed revival experts is that it is better to have revival with flaws—sometimes embarrassing, painful, and all too human flaws—than no revival at all.

Testing the Spirits Without Quenching the Spirit

Assessing revival is a difficult task. On the one hand, there are urgent biblical warnings against quenching and blaspheming the Holy Spirit. On the other, there are more numerous and equally urgent exhortations to be zealous for the truth, cautious about deception, and ruthlessly opposed to the devil, who can appear as an angel of light.

There is nothing in the Bible about how revival critics should conduct themselves, but Finney's "Revival Lectures" are full of negative references about naysayers. "The Spirit is grieved by saying or publishing things that are calculated to undervalue the work of God," he said. "Slandering revivals will often put them down."

And in a final urgent plea, Finney urged critics to exercise extreme caution:

> If Christians expect revivals to spread and prevail, till the world is converted, they must give up writing letters and publishing pieces calculated to excite suspicion and jealousy in regard to revivals, and must take hold of the work themselves.

Today videos and the Internet allow revivals like Brownsville to spread their message around the world. The same technology allows self-appointed critics to do likewise. Other than these developments in the methods of carrying on the debate, recent years seem to have brought little change in the ways believers battle believers over the question of how God works.

Changed Lives

On the move

Jeff and Alison Gardner, shown here with Brownsville pastor John Kilpatrick, are taking the message of revival around the country.

"He's Here!"

In the summer of 1995 the revival at Brownsville was still young, and its effects were still being felt mainly among longtime church members, many of whom were suddenly being woken from a lengthy spiritual lethargy.

Revival profoundly changed members of the Ward family, who had attended Brownsville for years. In July 1995, just a few weeks after revival began, high school student Amy Elizabeth Ward testified how God had transformed her from a lukewarm brat to a committed Christian.

In August it was nineteen-year-old college student Alison Ward who testified about what God had done to her after she heard evangelist Steve Hill preach on Luke 16:13 ("No servant can serve two masters"). Her testimony, which was videotaped by Brownsville's TV cameras, remains one of the pivotal moments of the entire revival.

Shaking so violently that pastor John Kilpatrick had to steady her behind the church's big pulpit, Alison described the various ways God had been touching her spirit. "He's here," she said, wincing as if she were being pelted with heavenly hailstones. "Sometimes the glory of God is so strong I can't really take it. It's like there are waves of God inside of me."

Soon Kilpatrick was overcome with the power of the Spirit himself. He let go of Alison and sank to a kneeling position next to the pulpit. Alison continued to speak, describing how God had given her a spirit of intercession for others as her voice grew weaker and as her shaking became more violent.

"It's painful to my heart," she said. "He is in a hurry. There's not much more time. He aches and He grieves for your spirit. He grieves for you."

Suddenly overcome herself, Alison fell in a heap behind the pulpit. As she did so, the sanctuary echoed with the sounds of people moaning and wailing. After a few moments, evangelist Steve Hill rose and told the crowd that he would not be delivering his usual sermon that evening. "This is the message tonight," he said. "The Word of the Lord has been preached." Hill invited people forward to get right with God as church member Charity James sang "Mercy Seat," a song of invitation that has become a revival staple. Soon hundreds of people were crowding the aisles near the altar.

By the next day church members and revival attendees were already distributing videos of Alison's testimony. And within days reports started coming in that the tapes were having a powerful effect on those who saw it. One young person who watched it said God used it to convict him of sin and bring him to repentance. A pastor who showed the video at a church service fell to the floor behind the altar. Youth groups around the country played it at their meetings, and startled youth pastors watched in amazement as previously hardened young people gave their lives to God.

Today, as she sits with her husband and ministry partner, Jeff Gardner, Alison remains surprised at the widespread impact the video seems to have had. "For some reason, God has used that video to touch people and show them His power," she says. "I don't understand how God can use a piece of plastic, but I know you can put pornography on a videotape, and people who watch that can destroy their lives."

Jeff, a minister with the Assemblies of God, is an employee of Steve Hill's ministry, Together in the Harvest. Jeff and Alison also travel and speak together about revival on their own. "Alison and I view our ministry as an extension of the revival," says Jeff.

Jeff grew up in church but had never taken Christianity seriously. He says he gave his life to God when he was sixteen. "God spoke to my heart and said, 'Love Me or hate Me, but no more games.'" Now he and Alison tell others about a vital relationship with God and the difference between that and a stale, stagnant "churchianity."

For Alison, the spotlight may have dimmed in the past three years, but her love for God has not.

"At first the revival was just a new and exciting thing," says

Alison. "Now it's a deeper thing. I've learned more about God, and the longer you know God, the more there is to know about Him."

Outbreaks like Brownsville are part of a much larger worldwide trend that has swelled the ranks of charismatic and pentecostal believers.

CHAPTER TWELVE

The Big Picture:

Brownsville's Place in the Work of God

As this book was heading to press in late 1998, the revival in Brownsville was continuing in full swing. People were still traveling to Pensacola from around the world. Crowds were still lining up outside the church hoping to get in. And those who did get in were adding to the already impressive number of reports about dramatic conversions and powerful life transformations.

But what will future historians say about Brownsville? Will it be seen as a small blip on America's sociocultural radar screen? Or will it, and related awakenings during the last quarter of the twentieth century and the beginning of the twenty-first, be honored as America's Third Great Awakening, a time when impressive numbers of Americans turned to God and stirred renewal throughout the world?

It is at least a century too early to tell. Many pundits have demonstrated the dangers involved in making long-range predictions about subjects as slippery as religion and spirituality.

Estimating how long the revival will last or how significant its impact will be is trickier than trying to take a snapshot of a speeding rocket. Focus in on one aspect of the phenomenon, and it speeds by and disappears from view. While the Brownsville revival is not moving at supersonic speeds, it still shows plentiful signs of youthful vitality, and its services continue to evolve, focusing on repentance and holiness one night before shifting radically the next to emphasize the closeness and tangibility of God.

Brownsville is still a long way from approaching the vast social and ecclesiastical impact of America's Great Awakenings, which have been employed as yardsticks in this study. Only time will tell how it measures up.

Still, tentative conclusions can be drawn. And unlike the previous chapters, which have provided detailed descriptions of various aspects of the revival, this chapter will explore some of its implications.

First, we will examine Brownsville's place within the broader context of one of the most important trends of our day: the phenomenal worldwide growth of pentecostal and charismatic Christianity. Next, we'll hear what Brownsville's leaders have to say about the movement they have been a part of. And finally, I will offer a few modest observations.

All this can help us assess Brownsville. But then again, everything could change tomorrow!

The Pentecostal/Charismatic Wave

In 1965 theologian Harvey Cox boldly predicted the demise of religion and the ultimate rise of secularism in his groundbreaking book, *The Secular City*. "The rise of urban civilization and the collapse of traditional religion are the two main hallmarks of our era," he wrote in the book's introduction, in which he prophesied the imminent "loosing of the world from religious and quasi-religious understandings of itself . . . [and] the breaking of all supernatural myths and sacred symbols."

This triumph of secularism, he wrote, would not merely be confined to North America, but was "spreading into every corner of the globe." As a result, people would need to begin speaking of faith in new, nonsupernatural ways, he said, adding, "It will do no good to cling to our religious and metaphysical versions of Christianity in the hope that one day religion or metaphysics will once again be back."

The ink was hardly dry on the first of the book's dozens of printings when the initial rumblings of the charismatic movement and the Jesus movement were beginning to be felt in the U.S. And over the next few decades, the world would see an incredible growth of interest in religion and spirituality. This growth, which one French writer called "La Revanche de Dieu" ("The Revenge of God"), would prove the utter ridiculousness of Cox's earlier projections of religion's demise.

By 1995 Cox was singing a far different tune. In his introduction to *Fire from Heaven: The Rise of Pentecostal Spirituality and the Reshaping of Religion in the Twenty-first Century*, Cox explored the rapid worldwide growth of pentecostalism. He also tried to explain (without necessarily apologizing) for his earlier errors. "Perhaps I was too young and too impressionable when the scholars made those sobering projections," he wrote. "Today, it is secularity, not spirituality, that may be headed for extinction."

People wanting to see examples of the pentecostal revolution Cox described could travel to Africa, Latin America, or Asia, where red-hot, Spirit-filled congregations were converting millions of souls while ushering in a new wave of New Testament-style deliverance, worship, visions, and miracles.

Of course, Americans who did not want to travel so far could visit Brownsville Assembly of God in Pensacola, Florida. The spiritual outpouring there broke out after Cox finished writing his book.

The Brownsville revival just barely made it into Vinson Synan's 1997 book, *The Holiness-Pentecostal Tradition*. This readable survey is a thorough revision of the author's 1971 groundbreaking work which, had it been read by Harvey Cox, could have alerted him to the revolution to come.

Synan, the dean of the School of Divinity at Pat Robertson's

Regent University, argues that pentecostal and charismatic varieties of Christianity are the fastest growing forms of the faith on the face of the earth. Starting with just a few dozen members in 1901, pentecostal and charismatic churches are projected to have over half a billion members worldwide by the year 2000. If these projections, developed by researcher David Barrett, come to pass, this means that pentecostal and charismatic believers will be the largest family of Protestant Christians in the world, outpacing the combined membership of Anglican, Baptist, and other Protestant traditions, but still lagging behind the worldwide Catholic communion, currently approaching an estimated one billion souls.

And it is not just card-carrying pentecostals who are causing this massive increase. Peter Wagner, author and Fuller Theological Seminary professor, coined the term *third wave* to describe the growing movement of evangelical Christians who embrace the gifts of the Holy Spirit and practice a deeper, more experiential faith, but do so without changing churches, and without embracing either the pentecostal or charismatic labels. Wagner argues that this third wave has been a powerful force in the worldwide growth of the church during the last quarter-century. "In all of human history, no other non-political, non-militaristic, voluntary human movement has grown as rapidly as the pentecostal-charismatic movement in the last twenty-five years."

The revival at Brownsville shows that old-line pentecostal churches can still play an important role in the ongoing spiritual revolution. However, Wagner's third-wave theory helps explain why hundreds of thousands of people who would not consider themselves pentecostal or charismatic have actively and joyously participated in the revival.

One such third-waver is Julie Frye, a member of a nondenominational evangelical church in Grand Rapids, Michigan, the Bible Belt of Reformed Protestantism. "I'm wanting to grow in the gifts of the Holy Spirit," Julie told me as she and nearly a dozen other Grand Rapids women in their twenties, thirties, and forties neared the end of their twelve-hour wait to get into a Brownsville revival service.

Julie's search for what many people in line call "more of the Lord" has taken her to a Vineyard conference in Columbus, Ohio, and to Toronto's Airport Vineyard church. She describes her experience at the Toronto church as "very weird," but she still believes the Holy Spirit was working there.

Although she is committed to her home church, which she says "is growing in the gifts of the Spirit," Julie says she will continue looking to places like Brownsville as spiritual oases. "I'm not accepting everything that is out there," she says, "but I do want everything the Lord has for me."

Like fellow believers in Africa and Asia, Julie is part of a dynamic spiritual movement made up of those who seek a faith that can be felt and experienced. It is a movement that pays little heed to either national or denominational boundaries.

In America, though, spiritual seekers looking for an experiential faith often conclude that such a thing cannot be found in any Christian church they have ever seen. They often wind up in cults, ashrams, or New Age encounter groups instead.

But at places like Brownsville, people say they can both *know about* God intellectually and *know* Him experientially. Or as *Newsweek* writer Kenneth L. Woodward put it in an April 1998 article, "Most Christians believe in the Holy Spirit . . . but it is the pentecostals who have transformed this belief into a body-rattling, soul-wrenching personal experience."

The vast majority of pentecostals, charismatics, and third-wavers would stare at you blankly if you told them their expression of the Christian faith was a barometer of changing religious climates in a postmodern age. But for many of them, their deep intimacy with God is a radical act of personal spiritual devotion in the midst of what they see as a faithless age. They swear by the ancient creeds of the church, but for them, creeds are not the soul of Christianity, merely its boundary markers. In their personal lives as well as in their joyous corporate worship, these believers are reaffirming the reality and the relevance of the supernatural in an age of widespread skepticism, naturalism, and materialism. And if you believe the experts, their pilgrimage to the heart of God represents one of the defining characteristics of our century.

The Inside Track

The leaders of the Brownsville awakening say it is not something they planned, even though they sought it and prayed for it for years. Most of the time, they say the revival is leading *them*, not the other way around.

Since the revival began in 1995, they have not had much free time for contemplation—or anything else. For most of the past three and one-half years, they have felt as if they're at ground zero of some huge religious explosion.

And Michael Brown, for one, feels like the commotion could continue until Christ comes again.

> There is no reason that this could not be part of a final series of waves of revival which will continue until the return of Jesus. That could be ten years, or it could be a hundred years. But if we cooperate with the Lord, the fires can keep burning.

Assemblies of God General Superintendent Thomas Trask agrees with Brown, at least in theory. "The Christian church can and should live in revival constantly," he says. "And I believe a congregation could do that." Still, Trask is betting that this revival, like all known revivals that have proceeded it, will come to an end some day. And he regularly reminds the revival's leaders to remain aware of that probability.

One of my cautions and one of my concerns is that there's a tremendous responsibility on pastor John Kilpatrick and Steve Hill that they don't try to perpetuate something that God wants to put a stop to. A day will come when [preparing for the revival's end] will have to be done.

Brownsville youth minister Richard Crisco is even more direct. "This revival will end," he says with conviction. "That's just common sense. It may be this year, or it may be ten years from now." And Crisco, who has seen the revival catapult him to nationwide fame among fellow youth workers, seems ready to return to anonymity. "I've always been satisfied being a nobody," he says, "and I'll be satisfied going back to being a nobody."

Pastor John Kilpatrick is not making any bets. For him, the continuation of the revival is a day-by-day experience of God's grace. "We take nothing for granted," he says. "We come in here every evening and say, 'God, will You visit us again?'"

As he scans the crowds that fill his church's sanctuary, Kilpatrick is looking for new faces. He regularly asks those who are making their first visit to the revival to raise their hands. It's one of the ways he tries to determine whether the revival is still fresh and vital or whether it's dead or dying.

We ask constantly how many people are here for the first time. That's an indication to us that this thing is not stalemated. If we see that sinners are not coming here, or that souls are not being saved, Steve and I will be gone and I will shut this thing down. We'll go home.

Anyone who thinks Kilpatrick is kidding needs to take a look at Brownsville's new sanctuary. The building, which is called the Family Life Center and sits across from the existing Brownsville sanctuary, seats twenty-five hundred. Many people had advised

Kilpatrick to build a new facility that would seat between seven thousand and ten thousand. And there are certainly times when revival-goers could fill a facility that large. But Kilpatrick, who is known for both his conservatism and his disdain for pastors going after "bigness," went small. "We didn't want to build some big albatross that, five years from now, people would drive by and say, 'My God! That's where that revival took place!'"

Lindell Cooley, Brownsville's energetic worship leader, is one of the more thoughtful and articulate artists in a field that is best known for musicians who sound eloquent when they're singing or playing an instrument, but who sound simplistic when they talk. Nor is Cooley fooled by the emotional power of music. He knows that a talented or manipulative artist can exploit people's feelings, making them believe they have had an encounter with God when all that's really happened is a well-executed rhythm or key change.

This skepticism about human nature, along with decades of experience on the sawdust trail, leads Cooley to disagree with Kilpatrick on one important point. As Cooley sees it, people could still continue flocking to Brownsville long after God's unique and temporary anointing has left.

> This revival won't be over just when the crowds are gone. This thing could be over a good six months to two years before the crowds quit coming. We need to look hard at ourselves and make sure we aren't perpetuating something God is finished with.

Cooley talks passionately about something a speaker once termed "The Five M's of Christianity." As Cooley explains, when God does a work with frail humans, He starts with an individual *man* (or woman). The second M is the *message* God gives that person to deliver. So far, so good.

But trouble begins when humans begin to develop *methods* (the third M) to channel God's work. Methods are not inherently wrong, and sometimes they are necessary tools for churches coping with growth and success. But the danger is that methods can replace a sense of dependence on God. Cooley says the apostle Paul warned believers to stay away from leaders who relied on methods rather than God, referring to them as people who have "a form of godliness but denying its power" (2 Tim. 3:5).

When methodology triumphs over true spiritual vitality, the result is a *machine* (the fourth M), which by definition is something that does the work once performed by a living being.

And as Cooley writes in his book, *A Touch of Glory*, the final stage of the process—the fifth M—is a *memorial*:

> My pentecostal brethren built a memorial to Azusa Street, and the Methodists built a memorial to the Wesley brothers. The Presbyterians memorialized John Calvin, and the Lutherans built their memorial for Martin Luther. All these things mark marvelous works of God on men, but do they also mark His conspicuous absence from our churches today?

As early as January 1998 Cooley was saying Brownsville was "dangerously close" to moving from the method stage to the machine stage. "This revival will end," he says with not a trace of uncertainty. And he believes that when the memorial to Brownsville is raised, its plaque might say something like this:

IN MEMORY OF THE BROWNSVILLE REVIVAL,
WHICH WAS A SMALL PIECE OF WHAT GOD WAS DOING
WITH HIS CHURCH IN THE LATE TWENTIETH CENTURY,
PARTICULARLY THE PENTECOSTAL CHURCH IN
SOUTHERN AMERICA

Evangelist Steve Hill's seven-hundred-plus revival sermons have enabled him to say more about what is happening at Brownsville than anybody else, and most of the time his assessment has been effusive. "I believe we're at the beginning of the greatest worldwide revival the world has ever seen," he said in one sermon. In another, he said: "This is called a move of God. For those of you who wished you had lived through one, welcome!" And in yet another sermon, Hill imagined God taking a look at the Brownsville revival and enjoying the show: "I've got a feeling that if there's a big-screen TV in heaven, He's got a remote and He's tuning in."

Most people figure that such remarkable statements are some kind of hyped-up evangelist-speak. But even when he's not in the pulpit, Hill is euphoric about the revival, he's thrilled to be involved in it, and he's convinced it's one for the history books. As he told me:

> I think that if this revival were to stop tomorrow, historians would conclude that it was the largest revival to ever spring from a local congregation. There have been more than two million people through here. Our Web site has had over five million hits. People from 110 nations have visited this revival. And our videos and audiotapes are being watched and listened to all over the world.

But like Kilpatrick, Hill takes nothing for granted, and he cautiously examines the faces of the people in the crowd for signs of whether or not "the dove has flown," which is Brownsville shorthand for the end of God's supernatural blessing of the revival.

> The one thing that would speak to me about the revival coming to an end would be if people stopped coming here with a hunger. But the intensity and the spiritual hunger of the people is as strong as it's ever been. People who come here and get fed go back to their cities and countries and tell others, "I have found food." That leads others to come.

Still, Hill acknowledges that things will not continue like this forever. "If this thing stopped, that's God," he says. "But we're not doing anything to fan the flame."

Hill can probably rest assured that Brownsville will at least be mentioned in future church history books. He is clearly excited about joining the ranks of all the heroes of the faith he has studied, but to him, that's not the main point.

> This revival isn't the most important thing to me. Jesus is the most important thing to me. And all that matters to me is whether this thing made a significant mark in the true church of the Lord Jesus Christ. Anyone would be pleased to be recorded in the history books, but what matters to me is whether this matters to God.

Concluding Postscript

For me, witnessing and writing about the Brownsville revival has been a rewarding and eye-opening experience. As a Christian for more than twenty-five years and currently a member of a vital Presbyterian congregation, visiting Brownsville has given me a fresh appreciation of the wonder of worship, a reminder of the powerful impact of bold, biblical preaching, and a deeper appreciation for the myriad ways God works in and through people's lives.

Getting to know the revival's leaders and having a chance to talk to some of the people whose lives have been transformed by it have been exciting and refreshing.

Still, I did not understand or like everything I saw during the revival services I witnessed. Interestingly, neither did the revival's leaders, who at times seemed just as confused, amazed, or frustrated by what was happening before their eyes. I'm not ready to become a card-carrying pentecostal, but I have a much clearer understanding of the rich and complex culture of this strong stream of American Christianity, as well as a deeper appreciation for the important contribution it has to offer the church.

I would like to visit Brownsville again in 2004 and see what's happening. If the revival is still going strong, it would be interesting to document its evolution. And even if the embers have cooled somewhat by then, it would be good to know what kind of lasting impact it has had on its host congregation, on the thousands of people who have been changed there, and on the many pastors and churches around the world who say it has renewed and revitalized their faith. It would be helpful to know what kind of difference Steve Hill's seven-hundred-plus sermons made, and whether the thousands who came to the altar were transformed in any significant and lasting way. I would like to find out how many of Michael Brown's students at the Brownsville Revival School of Ministry carried through on their commitment to spread the gospel throughout the world, and how many gave up, flaked out, or fell away.

For now, we know that Brownsville has been an unusually large and long-lasting, high-tech version of a centuries-old American-style revival. Brownsville has hosted more than two million people at services and has impacted millions more through local TV broadcasts, the Internet, and audio- and videotapes. These numbers alone ought to earn it a place in the revival hall of fame.

But numbers are not everything, and in some ways, Brownsville's numbers are not even that impressive. More people attend Rolling Stones concerts than participate in revival meetings in Pensacola. Greater numbers of people go online to shop or view pornography than log on to the revival's Web site. And within American evangelicalism, Brownsville is not even on many leaders' radar, a consequence, perhaps, of something Tim Weber calls "the balkanization of Christianity."

"I don't see many other people besides pentecostals and charismatics getting 'strangely warmed' over Brownsville," Weber told me, adding that "one wing of evangelicalism can get completely hot and bothered" about it, while "the other wing is not even breaking a sweat." With Brownsville, as with much more in contemporary Christianity, it seems that the right hand does not know what the left hand is doing; and that the church seems less like the body of Christ than a number of separate and self-sustaining organs or limbs.

The longer the revival continues, the more revival leaders are tempted to make extravagant claims about its significance. In June 1998 the revival passed the three-year mark—an important milestone indeed. But the following August, Steve Hill told me he believed the Brownsville revival was the biggest in American history. Coming from Hill, someone who knows and appreciates church history, the statement shocked me.

In fact, comparing Brownsville's numbers to those of the Great Awakening shows that Brownsville still has a very long way to go before equaling the impact of this and other earlier revivals. During his preaching tours of colonial America, George Whitefield was a nationally known celebrity who preached directly to an estimated 80 percent of the population. To rival that kind of impact and those kinds of numbers, Steve Hill would have to host a televised daily talk show, and he would need to preach to closer to two hundred million people, not the two million he has reached thus far!

Still, Brownsville seems destined to be more than a footnote in the story of the church, and it may well be viewed as a significant event in modern American religious history.

But is that all?

As Jesus neared the end of His Sermon on the Mount, He uttered these seven simple words: "By their fruit you will know them" (Matt. 7:20 NKJV). Spiritual fruit, like the natural kind, takes time to mature. The only real way to assess Brownsville's impact is to come back in five years—or a hundred years—and see what remains.

Appendix A

Sources

A number of books and resources provided me with helpful information and insight. Not all of them were cited, but they all helped me understand.

General Sources on Revival

An excellent source for people just starting out is *Christian History* magazine, which has published issues on "Spiritual Awakenings in North America" (Vol. VIII, No. 3), "Jonathan Edwards and the Great Awakening" (Vol. IV, No. 4), George Whitefield (Vol. XII, No. 2), Charles Finney (Vol. VII, No. 4), and John Wesley (Vol. II, No. 1).

Some of the classics on revival are available in affordable paperback editions, including an excellent collection entitled *Jonathan Edwards on Revival* (Banner of Truth, 1995) and Finney's *Revival Lectures* (Fleming Revell, no date). In 1997 Steve Hill's Together in the Harvest ministry published *The Azusa Street Papers*, which contains reproductions of the tabloid newspapers published by leaders of the revival that started the pentecostal movement.

Richard M. Riss's *A Survey of 20th Century Revival Movements in North America* (Hendrickson, 1988) is a helpful introduction to recent awakenings, while John Gillies's hefty *Historical Collections of Accounts of Revival* (Banner of Truth, 1981) contains some interesting details about older movements. David Edwin Harrell's *All Things Are Possible* (Indiana

University Press, 1975) is an excellent and readable overview of recent healing and charismatic revivals. Dennis Covington's *Salvation on Sand Mountain* (Addison Wesley, 1995), a moving portrayal of Appalachia's snake handling groups, is not really relevant to this study, but it does provide a praiseworthy model for combining journalistic instincts with compassion for wildly religious subjects.

Hank Hanegraaff is contemporary American evangelicalism's best known revival critic. His *Counterfeit Revival* (Word, 1997) misconstrues Jonathan Edwards, and it does not mention Brownsville. However, it does provide a frightening picture of various types of religious excess. For Hanegraaff material that does criticize Brownsville, contact the Christian Research Institute in Rancho Santa Margarita, CA (phone: 714/858-6100; fax: 714/858-6111).

When your eyes grow weary from reading about revival's excesses, pop *Elmer Gantry* into your VCR and sit back for a wild ride. This 1960 Academy Award-winning film's riveting performances illustrate the perennial tensions between awestruck believers and naysaying journalists, and warns that revival leaders risk falling if they begin believing their own PR.

Brownsville Sources

The leaders of the Brownsville revival have released numerous books. All are published by Destiny Image, unless otherwise noted.

In addition to hundreds of sermons (with many available in both audio- and video versions), Pastor John Kilpatrick has written two books. *Feast of Fire* (1995) is an intriguing spiritual autobiography. *When the Heavens Are Brass: Keys to Genuine Revival* (1997) focuses more on personal spiritual growth than church-wide renewal.

Many of Steve Hill's seven-hundred-plus sermons are available on audio- and videotapes. These tapes capture his compelling style much better than his books. Among the most popular videos are *White Cane Religion* and *The Hard Core Gospel*. For written versions of Hill's sermons, read his *The God Mockers* (1997), which contains his unique "you'ns" monologue. In addition, Hill's *Stone Cold Heart* (Together in the Harvest, 1995) is a powerful account of his conversion to Christ.

In the time it takes you to read this sentence, Mike Brown probably will have added another book to his growing body of work. *Let No One Deceive You* (1997) is a solid theological defense of the Brownsville revival. Inspired by Hank Hanegraaff's attacks, the book is more focused than 1996's *From Holy Laughter to Holy Fire*.

Worship leader Lindell Cooley tells his story in *A Touch of Glory* (1997), which gives readers a fascinating glimpse at a pentecostal childhood. And no matter what your religious persuasion, the *Awake America Live* recording is one smokin' album.

Youth pastor Richard Crisco's *It's Time* includes autobiography as well as insight on ministry.

There are hundreds of revival service videos available, most for ten dollars each. "The Father's Day Outpouring" shows how it all began in 1995. "Voice of Many Waters" features baptismal testimonies of those converted or renewed through the revival. Take your pick among the remaining hundreds: all feature rousing music and a Steve Hill sermon.

Most of the Brownsville books should be available at your local Christian bookstore. If not, they and many of the other materials can be purchased directly from the church's Distribution Center (phone: 850/438-2030; fax: 850/438-9246).

You can also access the church's Web page:
<www.brownsville-revival.org>

The *Pensacola News Journal's* November 1997 and 1998 investigative series, "Brownsville Revival: The Money and the Myths," is available at the paper's Web site: <www.pensacolanewsjournal.com>

Cathy Wood has been photographing and writing about the revival since the beginning. Her self-published *The Visitation: The Brownsville Revival* is a no-holds-barred first-person account of what this revival felt like and looked like to her. Copies are available for twenty dollars. E-mail her at SisterWood@aol.com or fax 850/937-0743.

Appendix B

Acknowledgments

I would like to thank some of the people who helped me write this book.

First, I would like to thank John Kennedy and Tim Morgan of *Christianity Today*, who dispatched me to Pensacola in 1996.

Greg Johnson of the literary agency of Alive Communications suggested this book and made the whole project happen. Janet Thoma edited with a seasoned combination of gentleness and firmness.

I couldn't have done any of this (and wouldn't have) without the cooperation of John Kilpatrick, Steve Hill, Lindell Cooley, Michael Brown, and Richard Crisco. All graciously gave of their time and their hearts, and permitted me to quote from their published materials.

Monte Unger's thorough and insightful research into revivalism was indispensable. And Cathy Wood, who witnessed the revival from the beginning, provided the photos that record this story in a powerful way.

Tim Weber and Vinson Synan read the manuscript, offered many helpful suggestions, and helped me avoid many stupid errors.

Lois, my loving wife, was, as usual, the best sounding board I could ever want.